Coffee Breaks
and
Birthday Cakes

Evaluating Workplace Cultures
to Develop Natural Supports
for Employees with Disabilities

David C. Hagner

Training Resource Network, Inc. • St. Augustine, Florida

First Edition

This publication is sold with the understanding that the publisher is not engaged in rendering legal, financial, medical, or other such services. If legal advice or other such expert assistance is required, a competent professional in the appropriate field should be sought. All brand and product names are trademarks or registered trademarks of their respective companies.

Printed in the United States of America.

Published by Training Resource Network, Inc., PO Box 439, St. Augustine, FL 32085-0439. You may order direct from the publisher for $29.00 plus $4.00 shipping by calling 904-823-9800 or visiting our Web site at www.trninc.com.

Library of Congress Cataloging-in-Publication Data
Hagner, David.
    Coffee breaks and birthday cakes : evaluating workplace cultures to develop natural supports for employees with disabilities / David C. Hagner.–1st ed.
        p. cm.
    Includes bibliographical references.
    ISBN 978-1-883302-31-3
        1. Handicapped–Employment. 2. Corporate culture. I. Title.

HD7255 .H24 1999
658.3′0087–dc21

99-045502

Contents

Part III
The Workplace Culture Survey 101

References 113

Appendix 117

The Workplace Culture Survey
   A. Strength of Workplace Culture
   B. Level of Workplace Inclusion

About the Author 123

Introduction

My Afternoon at the Greasy Spoon
By Flyonda Wall

I buzzed into the Greasy Spoon Diner about 1:30 for a late lunch. There were seven or eight customers inside, a pretty light day. The bus boy, cook assistant, and one waitress were sitting at their usual booth taking their lunch break together. They always sit at the same booth, and can choose from whatever is left over from the lunch menu, on the house.

Their conversation is fairly quiet and low key – not like yesterday when I observed in the back of the kitchen area, out where the supplies are kept and the door leads out to the Dumpster. They usually hang out there later in the day and that's when they're louder, and talk about the customers and complain about the job – stuff they can't get away with up front. Yesterday two waitresses were pushing and pulling each other off the bench, kidding and joking, while taking their 3:30 break back there.

Around 2:00 the manager yelled "Hey are you gonna sit there all day!" She was smiling though, and I think she was just teasing. This was her signal that lunch time was over for the three of them.

The manager, Jill, treats the workers like they are her family. Especially the waiters and dishwashers. Today she was showing Chris how to bus tables. His job is dishwashing but Jill had noticed that he was always curious about what was going on in the dining room, and asked if he would like to sometimes trade off and do the bussing.

She's like that with everybody. She treats the cooks a little more professionally, though – a little less casually. But she gives them whatever they ask for. "Without good cooks we might as well close the place," she says.

On her way back to the office Jill noticed that Ann, the new waitress, had forgotten to bring a customer his side-order. It was sitting there getting cold. Jill picked it up and brought it over to the customer. She never said a word to Ann. Everybody just pitches in and does what is needed. Later the cook teased Ann about it though.

All the waitresses carry beepers, and the cooks beep them when the food is ready. You can always see the beepers of the younger waitresses – they think it's cool to wear them right on the front of their uniform.

Rebecca, the older waitress, is talking to one of the regular customers. She is saying, "Yea, Jill does a great job. This place is run much better than it used to be." That's all I could hear of the conversation.

I decided to stick around all afternoon till closing time. Jill was going around to each person trying to figure out next week's schedule. She asks each person about what they want, and about their personal lives, making sure that everyone is happy about their schedule.

Dinner time was busy. When it's busy people don't talk much, only the stuff that's necessary to get the job done. They always greet and talk to the customers though. After dinner, at the end of the day, everybody pitches in with the cleaning. Jill is looking around inspecting the place. Oh no – gotta go! She has a fly swatter! AAAAAAhhh!

Part I

The Scope and Power of Workplace Culture

Every workplace has a culture, a set of shared meanings, expectations, values, and assumptions that govern what goes on at the workplace and how it is interpreted (Hatch, 1993). These meanings are reflected in observable symbols, customs, traditions, and artifacts at the workplace.

The concept of a "culture" began to be studied seriously in connection with work settings in the 1980s and has been widely adopted as a concept with important implications in the field of business management as well as in the sociology and anthropology of work (Hatch, 1993). Often the term "organizational culture" is used with reference to the culture of an entire company, which may consist of many different facilities and locations, while "workplace culture" refers to the aspects of culture that are unique to one specific setting.

As employees, we ordinarily don't give our own workplace culture much thought. We fit in so easily and comfortably that following our workplace culture's traditions and using its symbols has become second nature to us. For example, we know each day how to dress appropriately for work. Newcomers to our organizations quickly learn to arrive dressed correctly as either a manager or a line worker.

We may become more aware of the culture when we change to a new workplace, or when we experience a "culture shock." This is the occasional situation where someone violates the rules of the culture, such as coming to work dressed inappropriately for his or her role.

There are many different facets to a workplace culture. Some aspects of a culture may be written down, while others are unwritten. For example, a free meal for the employees of the Greasy Spoon Diner may be a formal policy of the company, whereas the fact that there is one particular booth waitresses always sit in when taking their break probably is an unwritten custom.

Only a part of a workplace culture will be formally or officially promulgated by the company. Most cultures have a great deal more to them. For instance, even if there is no written policy regarding proper dress, employees put a great deal of effort into their decisions regarding work attire (Rafaeli, Dutton, Harquail, and Mackie-Lewis, 1997).

Some aspects of a workplace culture are directly influenced by management priorities and style, while others are not. For example, at the Greasy Spoon Diner, Jill may have explained to the employees that she expects them to look out for one another and notice when someone may have forgotten something or need some help. But the practice of joking and teasing in the back room probably was never explicitly sanctioned or even noticed by the management; it just developed on its own.

Some cultures are stronger – they extend to more aspects of the setting and involve employees more fully – than others. As a rule, stronger cultures offer more possibilities for inclusion.

From the perspective of an individual employee, some cultures are a better fit or match than others. Very social people will not be happy in a setting where people keep to themselves. People who like getting dressed up for work will enjoy working around others who also like to pay attention to how they dress.

To some extent prospective employers seek employees who are likely to be a good match with the workplace culture, and prospective employees seek jobs in workplaces with workplace cultures that are likely to suit them. Once on the job, a process of adaptation further tests and refines the match.

Primarily, individuals adapt to the workplace. But to a lesser extent, workplaces also adapt to the individuals that make them up. The adaptation of workers to the workplace is much more noticeable for the simple reason that the workplace is usually there first and newcomers are usually a distinct minority. But situations arise where people move into a new facility, or a great number of new workers join an organization together. In those situations the individuals involved can create a culture, to some extent, to their specifications. Over time, every culture gradually evolves, in response to changes in circumstances as well as through the continual influx of new members.

This manual provides the tools to assess and understand workplace cultures. Specifically, it presents the Workplace Culture Survey, which explores thirty-one elements of workplace culture. You then can use this understanding to facilitate the selection and matching process and to better manage the inclusion of employees into the culture, particularly employees who are at risk of being excluded or marginalized. Looking carefully at workplace cultures is important because of the close connection between cultural inclusion and job success and job satisfaction, and because it has especially important implications for the increasing diversity of the workforce.

Workplace Culture and Job Success

By learning the workplace culture and fitting in with it, employees come to feel accepted by their co-workers and successful at their jobs. Inclusion in the culture is critical to job success because most work takes place in a social context. It is just as important for the waitresses at the Greasy Spoon Diner to "hang out" in back on break and joke with and tease one another as it is for them to perform their formal job tasks.

Why is this so? Why is participation in a workplace culture important even in areas that have nothing directly to do with performing the job? Work gets done not by individual workers completing their job tasks "independently," but by networks of workers mutually assisting and supporting one another. Informal alliances and support networks are critical to solving problems left unresolved and filling in gaps left uncovered by an employer's formal rules and structure (Morey and Luthans, 1991). No worker fully possesses all of the skills supposedly required "on paper" for his or her job position (Darrah, 1994).

Employees who are perceived by their supervisor as fitting in better with the work setting and work group, and who engage in such culturally meaningful behaviors as doing favors for or complimenting others, tend to receive higher ratings on their performance evaluations (Ferris and King, 1993; Wayne and Liden, 1995). The notion that one succeeds by "working hard" is true only if one keeps in mind that what it means to be "working hard" is unique to each particular workplace culture. At one setting, working hard might mean eating lunch at your work station most days. At another setting, it might mean turning in assignments ahead of time, regardless where one had lunch. At a third work setting, it might mean asking the supervisor for a new assignment when one has completed a previous assignment, regardless whether it is ahead of schedule or where one had lunch.

A great deal of the informal learning (Garrick, 1998) that goes on in the workplace consists of learning to negotiate the rules and expectations of the workplace culture. Sometimes we refer to the totality of work behavior, encompassing job task performance plus the additional social behavior related to fitting in with the culture, as "work role behavior" (Johnson, 1995).

Studies have consistently pointed to a failure to fit in socially as the primary reason for job loss. For example, Kennedy (1980) found that only about 25% of people who had a job loss failed because of not being able to perform the job tasks. The other 75% either were unable to get along with the boss (35%), were unable to get along with or win acceptance from their co-workers (25%), or could not go along with organizational values (15%). For whatever reason, they never became included in the culture.

Workplace Culture and Job Satisfaction

Another reason for looking carefully at workplace culture is that people, being social animals, build, maintain, and join cultures because they enjoy it. Thus, cultural inclusion is an important component of job satisfaction.

Employees tend to gravitate towards and select workplaces that have cultures conducive to their social preferences and styles (Wanous, 1992). Newcomers to an organization actively seek to understand the culture of the workplace and their role in it through observation and asking questions (Morrison, 1993). And the increased variety and broadening of perspective beyond one's own isolated job that comes from giving and receiving support and interacting socially with co-workers is viewed as a positive employment outcome by most employees (Campion, Cheraskin, and Stevens, 1994).

Each workplace culture is unique. People with previous work experience in a given field transferring to another work setting sometimes find the socialization process more difficult than those entering the field for the first time (Adkins, 1995). That is because they bring previously learned behaviors and understandings to the situation and gradually have to unlearn some of these to accommodate to the new culture. (This is one of the reasons why simulated work settings can never be as valuable for job training or preparation as real job settings.)

Workplace Culture and Diversity

People from diverse cultural backgrounds or who have characteristics that may stand out as different from other employees – for instance, age, ethnicity, gender, or disability status – sometimes need to pay particularly close attention to how they will fit in and join workplace cultures. This is because, first, some of their prospective co-workers may have been socialized and influenced by our wider culture to view people differently, depending on how they are categorized on these dimensions. Strategies will be required to counteract the tendency to maintain distance or to exclude these individuals from full participation.

Second, people who are less familiar with our culture (such as newly arrived immigrants) or less able to process cultural information (such as some individuals with intellectual or psychiatric disabilities) might benefit from active intervention to facilitate inclusion, such as guidance regarding what to look for, extra assistance learning what to do, or, depending on the culture, someone who can act as a "sponsor" to facilitate their inclusion.

As the diversity of the workforce increases, the need for strong workplace cultures also increases. A stronger culture is better able to include nontraditional employees, because it has within itself the capacity to facilitate connections and forge social bonds. And we will see that one of the hallmarks of a strong workplace culture is its potential for flexibility in responding to individual needs (Hall and Parker, 1993). It is something of a paradox that the same forces generating a strong sense of group identification also better allow people to be seen as individuals.

But while special populations benefit from a strong workplace culture, traditional employees also benefit. Akabas (1994) noted that the same conditions and circumstances that characterize a good place to work for employees at risk of non-inclusion also serve to define a good workplace for all employees. Akabas was writing specifically about employees with mental illness, but the same reasoning applies to other groups of people.

The degree to which a workplace can assimilate and support people at risk of exclusion is a test of its strength and health. Miners used to take a canary with them into the mines. If the canary died, it would be a sign that the air was unhealthy. Even though the miners could not directly detect anything amiss, they left the mine as fast as they could. Similarly, an inability of a workplace to tolerate or accommodate diversity is a sign that the work atmosphere may well be toxic for everyone.

It is important to distinguish between different kinds or levels of diversity. Harrison, Price, and Bell (1998) distinguished between *surface diversity* and *deep diversity*. Surface diversity includes differences among employees in characteristics like age, ethnicity, gender, and disability status. Deep diversity includes differences among employees in important values, attitudes, and beliefs.

Surface and deep diversity affect the workplace in opposite ways. Over time, the distancing effect of surface diversity tends to decrease. Workers come to know one another as individuals and come to view surface traits as less important. But over time the effects of deep diversity can become increasingly greater. Deep diversity can disrupt group cohesion, as people discover that basic differences in values, attitudes and beliefs make it difficult to share common goals and experiences.

Because strong cultures better accommodate diversity, the ability to analyze and work with workplace cultures can be of great value to people who provide various types of employment services. The term "employment service" or "employment service agency" is used here in its widest sense, to encompass an array of service types, including:

- community rehabilitation programs providing competitive employment assistance and follow-up and/or supported employment services to individuals with disabilities at community job sites;
- welfare-to-work organizations providing services such as job training, placement, and counseling for job success;
- school-to-work programs providing work-based learning, sponsoring internships or apprenticeships, or helping students with the transition to work; and
- company-based Employee Assistance Programs or human resource department assistance to employees experiencing a gender, ethnic, age, disability, or other barrier to employment success.

In a quality job match, the abilities and wants of the job seeker match job requirements and the culture of the workplace. Wanous (1992) conceptualizes this process as consisting of two separate but simultaneous matches:

1. The match of worker abilities to the task requirements of the job.
2. The match of worker interests and needs to the culture of the workplace.

Most employment services collect far more information about job seeker abilities and interests than they do about work settings. But it is not possible to match *any* two things without solid information about both sides of the match. Thus, it is critical that employment service personnel develop an expertise in assessing both the task requirements and the cultures of workplaces.

Although this may seem obvious, it often is ignored. For example, in supported employment, some employment specialists* sometimes focus exclusively on the job tasks a worker must perform. This is because they erroneously believe that job tasks constitute the complete job.

Other employment specialists understand the importance of social inclusion, but either have no strategies for facilitating it or believe that the use of facilitation techniques is counterproductive. They worry that they will ruin inclusion by the very fact that techniques are being imposed on the situation by the employment facilitator.

These employment specialists are wrong on both counts. There are techniques that can be useful for helping people join workplace cultures. If you are successfully employed, you probably used some of these techniques yourself, perhaps without being aware of it.

The situation in which an extra or outside person, the employment specialist, enters a workplace to facilitate inclusion by its very nature at least potentially brings in some degree of artificiality or stigma. And that tends towards social distancing rather than inclusion. But we will see that there are all sorts of ways to control and mitigate this unwanted side-effect of employment specialist intervention.

Ultimately, as with many other things, if one does anticipate that the disadvantages will wind up outweighing the advantages in a specific case, it would be wise to forego the external support of an employment specialist. But in most cases, the advantages outweigh the disadvantages. The alternatives to successful individualized employment are far more stigmatizing.

*the term "employment specialist" is used here as a general term covering direct employment service staff with these or similar job titles

Collecting Workplace Culture Information

Since the culture of each workplace is unique, it has to be figured out anew at each new worksite. How do you learn about the culture? Simply asking people to describe their workplace culture will not work. The participants in a culture are the experts in following the culture and fitting in with it, but they cannot necessarily explain it to you. Cultural information usually is obtained using multiple methods, over time, in three overlapping phases. (In Part II of this book, the specific elements of workplace culture examined by the Workplace Culture Survey are explored in depth.)

Phase 1: Job Development

The first phase consists of information collected by an applicant or job developer trying to determine if the workplace has a healthy culture or certain specific desired elements, prior to accepting a job offer. Only a partial analysis of selected elements of a culture can be obtained in this phase. But often this information is enough to determine if the company is worth pursuing further. A prospective applicant or job developer working on his or her behalf can obtain good information from several sources:

- from a social network contact person who has some "inside" knowledge about a company, such as a current or former employee. It is partly because information from these sources is so valuable that many successful employees report that they found their jobs through networking or personal contacts (Silliker, 1991);
- from company publications, brochures, annual reports, and web sites;
- from initial meetings and visits to the company for job development, job interviewing, informational interviewing, or job shadowing; and
- from sitting in on a company orientation session (element #10 of the Workplace Culture Survey).

Phase 2: Initial Training and Adjustment

In the second phase, you collect more information as you begin employment or gain access as an employment specialist assisting a new employee. This phase also applies to more extensive – two or more days in duration – job shadowing or job analysis visits. Information during this phase is collected by careful observation of the setting and workers, questioning and talking with workers, and "eavesdropping" or witnessing interactions engaged in by others. This type of data collection will reveal a great deal about a culture. For example, in the introductory narrative we are given Flyonda Wall's observations about the Greasy Spoon Diner. From these observations we can learn a number of things:

- There is a particular booth where waitresses, the bus boy, and the cook's assistant take their lunch break. They wait until they can take their break together.
- They take another short break later in the day, in the back of the restaurant. At this break people are louder, engage in a lot of joking and teasing, and say and do things that would not be allowed in the restaurant itself.
- Employees get a free meal during their shift as a job benefit.
- The manager notifies employees when their lunch break is over.
- The manager pays attention to employee preferences and interest in learning new jobs, and does some of the job training.
- People are expected to help one another out, especially if there is a food order that needs to be picked up.
- The younger waitresses wear their beepers conspicuously.
- Employees have a great deal of respect for the manager.
- To some extent, work schedules can be arranged to suit individual preferences.
- Everyone pitches in to complete the end-of-the-day cleanup.

Observation and witnessing interactions are relatively passive data collection methods. Questioning and conversing with workers is a more active strategy. A great deal of behavior is best understood by knowing the context of the behavior and how it is interpreted.

During the initial training and adjustment period one does not have the luxury of unlimited observation time to establish all the relevant contextual information. For instance, if one overhears a comment, was the comment meant to be serious or was it a joke? Questioning or interviewing must be used in conjunction with observation.

Usually these interviews are brief conversations with workers or managers about specific features of the culture, usually without using the word "interview," as it sounds too imposing and formal. Instead, try to adopt a role that Stern and Kaloff (1996) call the role of an "acceptable incompetent," and ask lots of naive questions. The individuals who provide answers and information become our "informants."

But observation and questioning during this phase still might not provide a complete picture of a workplace culture. One might encounter "on stage effects" (Stern and Kaloff, 1996) – situations where people act differently or unnaturally because you are observing or asking, or people being on their "best behavior" or giving you the surface or "official" version of how things are. Or people may deliberately hide pieces of their culture from view, usually because these pieces are unauthorized or problematic and are shown only to insiders or people who have patiently earned their trust. This level of cultural information is collected during Phase 3.

Phase 3: Ongoing Support or Follow-Along

Complete or practically complete information about a workplace culture can be achieved only by prolonged engagement, by visiting a worksite regularly enough to either be regarded as an insider in some capacity – as someone who belongs there – or to fade into the background of people's perception so that one isn't regarded at all.

The workplace culture we can know best is our own – where we ourselves are employed. Graham (1993) worked for one summer at an upscale country club restaurant, and during this extended time he became an insider. We can be sure of this because he was informed about several informal rules that would never be divulged to an outsider:

- If you drop a roll on the floor in view of a customer, apologize and throw it out; if you drop it in the kitchen, pick it up and put it back in the bread warmer.
- If a customer asks for decaffeinated coffee and you have no time to make it, use regular and add some water to cut the taste.
- If you are clearing a table and are 75% sure a customer did not use a particular utensil, put it back in the bin with the other clean ones.
- If you're making a sandwich on toasted bread and burn one side of the bread, serve it with the burned side in and some extra mayonnaise.

One can collect Phase 3 information without becoming employed at a worksite, through long-term involvement with a worksite as an employment specialist or employment consultant. Strategies appropriate at this stage are explained further in Chapter 3 in connection with completing the Workplace Culture Survey.

It is important to keep in mind that we never can claim that our knowledge of someone else's workplace culture is complete. One can always learn more. And as this learning is taking place, the culture is slowly changing. The process never ends.

Using Workplace Culture Information

We have all heard the old saying "knowledge is power." The knowledge of workplace cultures can be used in a variety of different ways by a variety of different people, including employment service staff, company managers, and employees themselves. It can provide a basis for understanding social inclusion and lead to powerful strategies for facilitating inclusion. It can equip an employee with the tools for maximizing success. And it can serve as a focal point for collaboration and partnership between an employment service and an employer.

Employment Service Staff

Workplace culture information can assist community rehabilitation or other employment service staff to develop jobs and support consumers at every stage in the employment process.

1. In a job search, job developers can survey the culture of a workplace along with analyzing jobs and learning about the needs of the employer. With this knowledge, an employment service more accurately can target work settings that match the social style and preferences of a job seeker and can steer clear of work settings likely to cause problems.

2. In negotiating with employers to establish a job position and negotiate the tasks, schedule, and other details of the job, employment service staff can be aware of and build connections to the culture for an employee. For example, they can make sure the job design allows the employee to take advantage of worksite gathering places (element #7 of the Workplace Culture Survey).

3. An understanding of the culture can suggest areas for employee training and other strategies for facilitating inclusion. For instance, a new employee may need to learn the key break-time customs (element #9). Employment specialists can consult with company personnel who will be doing the training, can teach the employee directly, or can find the combination of both strategies that best fits a particular culture.

4. As part of ongoing support, workplace culture information can be used to plan career development and job advancement

strategies. For example, a job in a company with a weaker culture might be developed for an entry-level work experience, followed by a transition to a job with a company that has a stronger culture and more possibilities for inclusion, support, and job satisfaction.

5. Workplace culture information can be used to design employment assistance strategies that are a good fit with the culture of a workplace and that take maximum advantage of whatever opportunities already exist in the culture for training and support.

6. Employment services that have inclusion as one of their goals can analyze workplace cultures and then evaluate the degree to which their consumers are included in the culture of a workplace or the progress in increasing the level of inclusion over time for an individual.

7. An understanding of workplace culture can become the basis for consultation with an employer on making improvements in a workplace culture that will benefit all employees.

8. An employment service can look internally, at its own workplace culture, and identify improvements that will increase the effectiveness of the service in carrying out its mission.

Managers and Management Consulting

Companies have found that information about workplace culture can be extremely valuable in helping meet their business goals. *US News and World Report* (Koerner, 1998) reported that about 40% of all consulting work by professional anthropologists involves not studying remote societies or ancient civilizations but consulting with the business world on workplace culture issues.

A healthy culture and positive co-worker relationships lower personnel costs and translate into higher productivity, better customer service, and increased sales. Knowledge about workplace cultures can be used by a business to:

1. create a realistic job preview (Wanous, 1992) that will allow prospective employees to have some understanding and feel for the culture in the job application phase and thereby improve the quality of job matches and decrease job turnover;

2. improve the orientation program at a company and devise strategies for better assisting new employees in becoming acclimated to and comfortable with the workplace culture;

3. design an internship or apprenticeship program that successfully bridges the transition to work and allows a firsthand look at prospective permanent employees;

4. improve a company's response to diversity in the workplace and increase the chance for success for members of groups that have traditionally been underrepresented; and

5. audit the workplace culture to diagnose problem areas and planning improvements in a company's operation and in employee job satisfaction, and over time to evaluate the success of efforts to build a healthier, more productive culture. This is perhaps the area in which businesses have the most to gain. For example, one company was attempting to improve product quality by investing heavily in a new training program, without success. It finally realized that "turf wars" between departments, not inadequate training, was behind its quality control problems. The problem could be resolved by focusing on this aspect of the workplace culture (Darrah, 1995).

Changes that enhance a workplace culture can be difficult to manage successfully. There is an ecological balance to a workplace, such that a culture cannot be changed through a frontal assault. It can only be weakened that way. Strengthening a culture is achieved by carefully nourishing and building upon existing positive features. Therefore, a detailed understanding of a workplace culture is an essential part of an organizational change strategy.

Employees and Job Applicants
Knowledge of workplace culture can be directly useful to a job seeker investigating employers and deciding how to respond to a job offer. It also can be useful to an employee wishing to improve his or her job satisfaction or chances for success in a job.

Employment service consumers can be shown how to analyze workplace cultures and thus take charge of their own inclusion planning. This method sometimes can make a critical difference in situations where a consumer does not wish to disclose a disability to the employer, for instance, yet will require some specialized supports.

Some techniques available to employment service staff for collecting cultural information without being on-site, or without one's presence being associated with the focal employee, are covered in Part III. But there also will be situations in which there is no way for an employment specialist to collect cultural information without the data collection itself acting as a disclosure. In these situations, the employee must become his or her own data collector and implement inclusion strategies on his or her own initiative.

Part II

The Elements of Workplace Culture

In Part II, workplace culture is broken down into thirty-one elements. Not every element is found at every workplace, but it is important to look for and assess each element. Some elements will be far more important than others at any given worksite.

For each element of the culture we first will frame a question that can be used to assess whether the element is present or relevant at a particular workplace culture. Second, we will consider how the element acts as a contributor to the culture as a whole and its relationship to other elements. Third, examples of the element are provided, as well as any tips or considerations for assessing the element. Fourth, some strategies are suggested that relate to providing employment assistance to a specific job seeker or employee* by either external support people such as supported employment service staff or internal support people such as human resources or affirmative action staff. And finally, we will consider the more system-level implications of the element from the perspective of company management or the provision of consultation to company managers.

The first step in analyzing a workplace culture is to specify the "workplace." This can be trickier than it seems. For small companies, in one location, like the Greasy Spoon Diner, the entire company is the workplace. However, the work of a company may be divided into two or more very distinct parts – for example the production area and the office area – so that each can be considered as having its own culture. In a larger company, often a "department" – accounts receivable, shipping and receiving, buildings and grounds, the mailroom, and so on – is the best unit of analysis. But a large department, or one that spans two floors of a building, may be thought of as more than one workplace. Any different location, such as a separate plant or store, is always its own work setting. There is often no one "correct"

*The terms "the employee" or "the focal employee" are used here to refer to this individual.

designation of a work setting. The key issue is consistency – maintaining the same possibly arbitrary workplace demarcation throughout the analysis.

Once the work setting is specified, all questions refer to that environment and the workers in it. Sometimes several questions cannot be answered in one way. The answer might be one thing for some employees but something else for other employees. This is a sign that the "workplace" is really more than one work setting and you should consider a particular subarea.

A description of each element of workplace culture follows. For each element, we look at Assessment, Implications for Employment Assistance, and Implications for Management and Management Consulting. The third topic is directed at managers of the company employing the supported worker. An employment specialist can become a valued asset to businesses by passing on this advice to them.

The question that leads off each element discussion corresponds with the question in Part A of the Workplace Culture Survey (page 117).

The Elements of Workplace Culture

1. Longevity
2. Joint Tasks
3. Shared Tasks
4. Co-Worker Help
5. Work Schedule
6. Social Times
7. Gathering Places
8. Mealtimes
9. Breaktimes
10. Orientation
11. Employee Training
12. Initiation Pranks
13. Special Terms and Jargon
14. Items Issued to Employees
15. Shared Equipment
16. Dress and Appearance
17. Name Display
18. Work Space Personalization
19. Social Interactions
20. Group Customs
21. Staff Meetings
22. Performance Review
23. Pay Distribution
24. Celebrations
25. Company-Sponsored Social Activities
26. Outside Activities
27. Employee Assistance and Wellness Programs
28. Car Pooling/Transportation
29. Employee Incentives
30. Work/Family Policies
31. Opportunities for Advancement

ELEMENT 1: LONGEVITY
Have most of the workers been with the company for a year or more?

Cultures are formed and maintained when people find themselves in the same situations, with the same people, encountering the same problems on a regular basis. The longer their association, the more customs and symbols they invent, and the more extensive their expectations about one another become.

People also tend to stick around stronger workplace cultures for longer periods of time. Transience indicates a weak culture. Thus, longevity is both an effect and a cause of workplace culture.

Another relationship between culture and longevity is that old-timers have a better chance of making their mark on a culture than newcomers. New people have to become included with those already there, rather than the other way around. Longevity gives one the upper hand. For instance, some workers use longevity as a sort of automatic job carving mechanism, because more senior workers gravitate towards tasks they prefer and give their less desired tasks to those with less seniority.

Assessment

The one-year point is selected arbitrarily to allow a "yes/no" answer to this question. A one-year or more tenure for most workers indicates a sufficient degree of stability to allow a strong culture to flourish. The job tenure of workers in many workplaces is of course a great deal longer.

Managers or human resource personnel usually can give a pretty good idea of the turnover rate at a company. The rate also can be estimated by asking several workers how long they have been with the organization. For this assessment, the total job tenure of an employee in any and all jobs that involve interactions with or exposure to the work setting should be included.

One might be able to sense a high turnover rate at a work setting if, when asked about their work, workers seem to psychologically distance themselves or define themselves as occupational transients (Pierce, 1996). They might say, "This isn't my real job" or "I'm just doing this until something comes up." Low longevity – high turnover – is common in a great deal of entry-level, low-salaried, low-benefits service work. A visitor literally might find new people on duty on each visit.

While some occupations seem to have a higher turnover than others, there is substantial variation across individual workplaces. One cannot make longevity assumptions on the basis of the occupation or type of work. As a rule dishwashers have a low level of longevity, but it is certainly possible to find restaurants where the dishwashing staff have been stable for years.

Implications for employment assistance

The fact that jobs where longevity is greater tend to have stronger cultures has important implications for job development. Some employment service job developers deliberately focus their efforts on companies with high turnover. The reason is fairly obvious: More job openings are found that way. But this means that customers of these services, possibly at a greater than usual risk of non-inclusion, are relegated to precisely those jobs in which there is less to be included in and less assistance available to facilitate inclusion.

Our outcomes will be far better if we "find the job for the person" rather than "find the person for the job." First, identify an individual's aspirations, plans, and job specifications. Then, assist the individual to contact companies with work that matches those as closely as possible. Networking, using a job seeker's family, friends, and other community contacts (including employment service staff) is the ideal way to identify potential employers. This way, the individual can gain access to a greater variety of companies and work settings than by relying on one or two professional job developers to generate leads (Lin and Dumin, 1986). High-turnover, weak-culture jobs are best thought of as short-term options to provide immediate income, to build a resume and obtain an employment reference, or to learn skills that will come in handy in the next job search.

Keep in mind, in connection with length of time on the job, that a person never can count on becoming better included in any work culture – weak or strong – solely as a function of time. This sometimes does happen, but an employee and by extension also an employment specialist never can count on it. Plan and systematically implement specific inclusion strategies or interventions. Sometimes the term "natural support" is mistakenly used to refer to the support that occurs in the absence of any intervention. But natural support also should include support that is facilitated; i.e., provided as a result of staff intervention, as long as it is provided by those who typically are present in the setting and is not viewed as unusual.

Implications for management and management consulting

High employee turnover, often a symptom of a weak or unhealthy workplace culture, is enormously expensive for a firm. Pfeffer (1998) calculated the savings to a company of 5,000 employees in reducing turnover from 20% to 3% at about $50 million a year. Most companies will receive tangible benefits from efforts to strengthen the culture in the form of lowered personnel costs due to turnover. Because longevity is partly an effect or result of inclusion, improvements in any of the other thirty elements of workplace culture will maximize the chances for longevity for an employee.

ELEMENT 2: JOINT TASKS
Are there some tasks that two or more workers perform together?

Working relationships form and interactions take place as employees participate in the production workflow with one another. The most direct way this happens is through two or more workers performing a task together as a member of a pair or team. Relationships and interactions are the glue that holds a workplace culture together. Most people enjoy the company of others. The impulse to engage in joint tasks is so strong that workers sometimes work together on a task even when they are getting in one another's way or when they are assigned to separate jobs.

Assessment

A joint task might look like this: Several workers unload a new shipment of stock. One worker lifts each box down to a second worker, who places it on a pallet and calls out the control number to a third worker, who checks it off the shipment manifest. Cleaning up at the end of the shift is a joint task at the Greasy Spoon Diner, because everyone pitches in and divides the task among themselves. Very isolated and very compartmentalized jobs may provide few or no joint tasks.

Joint tasks may occur infrequently (e.g., once a month), so direct observation over a short time period may miss them. One or two joint tasks might be relatively obvious to a casual observer, but analyzing all of the job positions in a work setting is the best way to identify all of the joint tasks.

Implications for employment assistance

Inclusion is enhanced when one or more joint tasks are an essential part of a worker's job. At some workplaces, it is natural for a novice to adopt a helper relationship with an expert. Thus the two of them will engage in a series of joint tasks. For example, a machinist might finish machining metal parts and pass them to a helper who packs them in crates for shipment.

Some jobs are designed in too isolated a way, without any joint tasks. If so, look for places in the workflow where jointly performing some task might fit easily with each person's job and improve the efficiency of the operation. Then either you as the employment specialist or the workers involved can suggest this job modification to the supervisor.

In joint tasks, each worker has a responsibility to keep up his or her end. Co-workers may become irritated at someone who always offers to lift the lighter side, or cleans less than his or her fair share of the area. A supervisor may welcome assistance in establishing a reasonable production expectation and timeline for improvement based on an employment specialist's knowledge of the training process. One also can model or coach co-workers if necessary in giving reminders or feedback, including complaints, to an employee.

It may be necessary to explain an employee's learning and support needs to a supervisor or co-workers in a way that discloses information about an individual's disability. If possible, a discussion of the issues this raises should take place with the individual or guardian prior to commencing job development. An employer should have access to any functional, work-related information about an employee's learning style, potential sources of stress, or physical capacities that directly relate to providing adequate training, support, supervision, and accommodations. Information about such things as diagnoses and disability labels, psychosocial history, and service planning is not directly relevant. As with any personal information that is not directly related to the job, an employee has the freedom to disclose as much or as little of this information as he or she wishes.

Implications for management and management consulting

If some discretion is allowed employees in designing or rearranging tasks, they may come up with ideas for joint tasks that will raise morale and job satisfaction as well as productivity. Placing relatively more emphasis on achieving production outcomes and relatively less emphasis on carrying out specific work processes, though both may be important, promotes co-worker cooperation and a climate of creative problem-solving.

Teamwork can breed conflict as well as collaboration. Therefore employees may require training in such topics as problem-solving, communication, team decision-making, and conflict management in order to be successful at joint tasks (Wellins and George, 1991). Many community rehabilitation and other human service programs assisting employees have a wealth of expertise available and can conduct training of this kind that will benefit the workforce as a whole.

ELEMENT 3: SHARED TASKS
Are there certain tasks at work that almost everyone does?

Culture emerges as people share places, things, and experiences. The more that are shared, the more participants can compare notes, commiserate or celebrate together, trade stories, and discuss strategies for dealing with what goes on. Shared tasks are tasks one worker performs that other workers also perform. When performed together as a team, these are joint tasks (element #2). But there are other tasks more than one person may do although they do not do them together.

When people share one or more tasks, they have at least that much in common and can identify with one other to at least that extent. They have something to talk about. The equipment, supplies, and setting act as props, or what sociologists call "discourse markers" (Henning, 1998). They focus and ground the conversation. For example, if two office employees share the use of one fax machine, one worker might remark, "Boy, that fax machine has been acting weird lately." The fax machine is then the focus for an interaction. Working relationships can begin in this way.

Assessment

Sending and retrieving faxes, getting supplies from the storeroom, and signing in and out are examples of tasks workers in an office might share. At the Greasy Spoon Diner, all the waitresses deliver orders to and pick up food from the cook. More than one job position with the same job title will be a strong indication of shared tasks across all of the employees with the same job title. Another, smaller set of tasks may be shared across many job positions.

Analyzing the tasks of several job positions will identify shared tasks. Analyzing the departmental work flow also will identify any other situations in which two or more people perform the same operation. Workflow is analyzed by tracing an operation's inputs through the process to its outputs. In a machine shop, machinists drills holes in metal plates for mounting electric motors. How do the plates get to the machinist? What happens to them once they are finished? What happens to the scrap metal that is accumulated in the process? It may be that each time a new box of materials is taken onto the shop floor the inventory clerk has to be notified, and so on. Analyzing the work flow in this way will identify the tasks that one or more employees share.

It is often useful to diagram the work flow, starting with incoming materials and ending with outgoing products, noting each key work process. In the case of product manufacturing, such a diagram will be relatively straightforward. But what about a service operation? The same sort of analysis applies to a real estate appraisal business, for example. Job orders, phone calls, and home inspection data come in. Appraisal reports go out. Examples of possible shared tasks are using the computer map software and preparing reports for overnight delivery mailing.

Implications for employment assistance

It is important to look for jobs that contain one or more shared tasks or ways that an isolated job can be enriched or enlarged by adding one or more shared tasks. To count as shared, tasks do not have to have any particular interactions. Just the fact that they are shared creates an unstated bond among the participants. However, the social benefits are maximized when the employee can participate in communication exchanges that relate to the shared tasks. The workplace itself contains props that relate to the shared tasks, for example, the fax machine and the inventory sheet. This makes it easy to use alternative and augmentative communication strategies, such as pictures, sentence cards, or sign language signs for workers whose use of language is limited.

Implications for management and management consulting

A division of labor in a business or department draws upon the unique assets and talents of each employee. But it is wise to leave a few tasks undivided. The old "Taylorist" model, whereby each employee performs only one or two discrete work tasks, is out of date. It has been replaced by an emphasis on cross-training and self-directed work teams. At the Greasy Spoon Diner, for instance, Ann was observed cross-training Chris, the dishwasher, so he would know how to bus tables. This type of management philosophy improves the workplace culture. It also provides more security of coverage during employee absences due to sick time, vacations, and turnover. The wider perspective each employee gains of the entire operation also increases employee problem-solving capacity and commitment to the company.

Cross-training and multi-task assignments will greatly increase the shared task linkages at a worksite. Given any set of employees and any set of work tasks, an increase in the number of tasks any worker performs always will result in an even greater increase in shared tasks for the work group as a whole. Take the simple example of a work setting with six workers and four tasks. Suppose that Workers One to Four share Tasks One and Two, Worker Five performs Task Three, and Worker Six performs Task Four. The total number of task sharings is eight (four workers share Task One and four workers share Task Two).

If Workers One and Two learn to perform one additional task each, say Task Five, the total number of task sharings increases by three to eleven (four share Task One, four share Task Two and three now share Task Three). In this way, cross-training can pay for itself many times over.

ELEMENT 4: CO-WORKER HELP

Are co-workers generally available to give help or support if a worker has a problem?

This element refers to the availability and proximity of assistance, if a worker needs it. To be of use, help has to be actually available, not merely theoretically. That means that there must be people close enough by to be called upon. There also must be a willingness and ability to help. Co-workers can either be formally required to give assistance, or co-worker help may be an informal workplace custom.

Networks of mutual support serve several functions. They allow the stronger and weaker skills of individual workers to balance one another. They fill in gaps, inconsistencies, and unforeseen circumstances in the way jobs are formally defined. And they develop personal relationships that make the work day more rewarding and satisfying.

In a network of mutual support, there is a general expectation that support be a matter of give and take. Giving help is like making a deposit in one's social support bank account. Receiving help is like making a withdrawal. There is no need or requirement for individual deposit and withdrawal amounts to match exactly. One can owe someone two favors, for example. But one cannot get too far in debt without running into serious trouble.

Assessment

There are two types of workplace culture that provide little or no co-worker help. The first is a culture of radical autonomy, where needing assistance is viewed as a weakness and workers experiencing a problem are governed by the rule "You're supposed to figure that out for yourself." The second is a very scattered or individualized type of work setting where co-workers are not around to help, as in the case of a night cleaner, or their availability is too sporadic to be relied upon. Some types of service work are performed in isolation because the operation is necessarily behind the scenes or after hours, such as most cleaning work. A worker assigned to such a job may be literally "invisible" (MacDonald and Siriani, 1996) and unable to access help.

Help and support usually are given not routinely or on a schedule – in which case they would be more appropriately viewed as joint tasks (element #2) – but on an episodic or as-needed basis. Thus observation cannot uncover the depth and scope of co-worker help unless the observation takes place over many months. It is best to engage workers in brief conversations, and ask what kinds of things they might need help with and what happens when they need help.

Support can be divided into two basic kinds. First, support may be instrumental, or practical, such as help lifting a heavy object or getting a ride in to work. Trach, Beatty, and Shelden (1998) have divided instrumental support into several functional subcategories:

- organizational – support in the preparation and organization of work, such as schedules, order of tasks, and location of materials;
- physical – changes in the design and function of physical objects and equipment at work; and
- training – skill development through direct instruction.

Their study was focused specifically on employees with disabilities. However, they found that employers do not view the supports provided to employees with disabilities as different from those provided to other employees.

Second, emotional or affective support involves such things as assisting someone to calm down when they are upset, or letting someone at work know that his or her contribution is appreciated. Affective support is helpful in a different way than instrumental support, but it can be as important or more important. Many direct service jobs such as cashier or receptionist, for example, entail a great deal of "emotional labor," such as appearing pleasant in the face of a rude customer. Affective support can be particularly critical in this type of situation. Often different co-workers are sources of different kinds of support.

Implications for employment assistance

It is important to be sure that an employee can communicate his or her needs to others and ask for help. For an individual who does not speak or use the same language as his or her co-workers, this communication can be through picture cards, signing, augmentative communication devices, or another method. Employment specialists find that often a supported employee will approach *them* with a problem. Unless the problem is unrelated to the job or legitimately involves very specialized human service expertise, it is best to show the individual which person in the work setting they should ask and how to go about it, rather than to solve the problem. Solving the problem for the individual fosters dependency. If an individual is not able to notice or communicate a need for help, there may be someone in the setting who could learn how to spot the need for help and how to respond.

For instance, in one factory setting a co-worker learned to recognize when Sally was becoming frustrated and to go over and see what was wrong.

Co-workers who are supporting an individual with a disability may in turn need support themselves. Co-workers have to feel capable and confident in giving help. One can enlist co-workers by identifying a support function readily within the individual's power that does not impose an undue burden. Then, as with any behavior one wants to increase, make sure the behavior of giving support is rewarding for the individual. The role of an employment specialist is to maximize help obtained from within the setting up to the point where it is perceived as a burden or becomes stigmatizing and thus counterproductive. Be careful not to "deputize" co-workers as resident job coaches or job coach aides. Their assistance should resemble and be viewed as not significantly different from the help any worker might give another.

Sometimes an employment specialist is unsure whether to ask company personnel to get involved in giving support in situations where no other employee would need a similar kind of support. For example, an employee needs help counting change from a lunch purchase. In one sense this is not like the help any one worker might give another because all the other workers can count. But the fundamental issue is how the support is perceived. Everyone's support needs are unique. One worker has an old car that keeps breaking down. Another can never remember to turn in production reports. A third is always becoming distressed by the ups and downs of romantic relationships. Each person in his or her unique situation is supported "just like everyone else." If assistance with change is viewed very differently, as "off the scale" or radically unlike other types of support people get, then it is better to treat it differently. Have the individual hire a part-time aide to assist with change at lunch, for example. But this seldom will be necessary. An increasing diversity of support needs is a natural and inevitable by-product of increased workplace diversity in general, and something healthy workplace cultures readily can accommodate.

Sometimes employment specialists employ a strategy known as "permission to be natural." This strategy neutralizes the tendency some co-workers or supervisors may have to treat an employee with a severe disability differently or to defer to the employment specialist to intervene in a problem situation that the co-worker or supervisor would ordinarily handle. The strategy is simply to ask the individual what approach he or she would ordinarily take, and legitimize it by concurring that it is an excellent approach (assuming that it is OK).

It is also important to help employees recognize how and when to offer help to their co-workers and notice when it is needed. People coming to work from a situation of relatively greater dependency (e.g., rehabilitation program, school, welfare) may sometimes expect that people either will intuit their need for help or may not realize the need to reciprocate.

It is customary to express appreciation for help freely given. Thus it may be necessary to prompt or teach employees how to show appropriate appreciation for help provided.

Implications for management and management consulting

Nothing builds teamwork and cooperation among the members of a work group more than a spirit of mutual assistance. Assign people to do things in pairs or groups in which each person's strengths and weaknesses balance one another.

It is a good idea to have helpfulness to co-workers as an item on everyone's performance evaluation (element #22).

If an individual has complex or multiple support needs because of a severe disability, use a "divide and conquer" strategy: Go through the worker's shift and list each specific support in functional terms. This is good to do at a group brainstorming meeting. For personal support, ask who the most logical person is at that point. One also can call upon rehabilitation engineering or assistive technology professionals for assistance with physical supports. State assistive technology projects can be a source of referral for this assistance.

ELEMENT 5: WORK SCHEDULE
Is there a set work schedule?

Physical proximity over a period of time is a precondition for building and maintaining a workplace culture. The same experience of getting up early, working a long day, and so on acts as a bond between people and sparks interactions. Other things being equal, a similar work schedule shared by at least some of the workers will be associated with a stronger culture.

Assessment

A high level of matching schedules means that most people's work times and work days coincide completely. When this element is missing, or nearly so, workers come and go independently of one another or on no set schedule. An example might be route salespeople who leave and report back at different times. (These individuals will form relationships and elements of culture with their customers that are very similar to co-worker relationships). The important things to look for are start and stop times, break and meal times, and employees' weekly schedules of days on and off.

Implications for employment assistance

As much as possible, arrange supports so that an employee's job is for the same full shift as his or her co-workers. For instance, in scheduling a school-sponsored work experience that will be linked with school-based learning, working two or three full days and attending a full day of school for the remaining days is preferable to working five half-days and attending school five half-days.

Often factors external to the work itself constrict or dictate an employee's work schedule and interventions are required. If bus transportation is at the wrong times or undependable (see element #28), carpooling with a co-worker might be a possibility. Also the need to retain public benefits, especially medical insurance, causes some people to restrict their hours of work. Work incentive provisions should be used creatively to reduce countable earned income below a level that would jeopardize needed benefits (Sheldon and Trach, 1998). If an individual's hours of work per month need to be lower than would be typical of those in a work setting, scheduling an extra day or two off per month is preferable to scheduling a shorter work day. If for some reason it is not possible for an employee to work the same full shift as his or her co-workers, it is important to include either the beginning or end of the shift, (i.e., arrive late or leave early, but don't do both) as well as break times (element #9) and more social times (element #6).

Implications for management and management consulting

If the type of business and production needs lend themselves to separate shifts or erratic schedules, try to build in some schedule overlap. Hospitals commonly schedule the first shift from 7:00 a.m. - 3:30 p.m., and the second shift 3:00 p.m. - 11:30 p.m. This leaves the 3:00 p.m. - 3:30 p.m. period for communication across shifts. Or, try to build in some weekly time when all employees can meet and connect with one another. For example, a preschool with separate Tuesday and Thursday teachers and Monday, Wednesday, and Friday teachers schedules a 90 minute staff meeting every Monday afternoon and requires the Tuesday/Thursday teachers to attend.

If neither of these suggestions can be implemented, some form of "virtual contact" by means of cell phones or e-mail – possibly an employee listserv – can establish a sense of connectedness among the team.

ELEMENT 6: SOCIAL TIMES

Is there a time during the work shift when it is easier or more likely for workers to talk socially?

Many social interactions at work are brief comments or exchanges that take place as people work near one another or perform joint tasks. Other times two jobs may intersect, such that a work-related interaction is required. For instance, waiters and waitresses must deliver food orders to the chef. The work-related interactions in these instances might "spill over" into something social.

Additionally, some shifts might have production "peaks" – requiring full or intense concentration on work – and "valleys" – when work slows down a little and workers can catch their breath. Social exchanges might tend to cluster around these "valleys," as workers take the opportunities that present themselves during these slower periods to interact socially, through brief exchanges or conversations.

Assessment

Some examples of production "valleys" might be between the busy meal times at a food service establishment, or the afternoon at a bakery. In a factory, sometimes work slows down a little when machinery is turned off for cleanup at the end of shift. This element will be absent or nearly so if the work pace demands intense concentration the whole day, such that the entire day is one continuous "peak." Also, if people are physically isolated or isolated by a barrier such as a high noise level, the only social times will be during designated breaks (element #9). But even under these conditions some brief social interactions (element #19) may be evident throughout the shift.

Implications for employment assistance

If for any reason an employee will not be able to work the same full shift as his or her co-workers (element # 5), employment specialists should work to ensure that the work schedule covers any identified social times.

It is important to understand to what degree and under what circumstances employees are free to talk while working during slower times. At some settings it is acceptable to make social comments only if this can be done while continuing to keep up the required work pace and productivity. At other settings there are informal customs governing the amount of time one can stop working to make a social comment or two before one risks getting into trouble. Or workers may be aware of the need to look busy in certain circumstances.

Many aspects of workplace culture are governed by complex rules and subtle discriminations like these. Learning only part of a custom or a simplified version of a custom can be dangerous. It may be necessary to learn the custom in detail to make a judgment as to whether it can be usefully taught to an employee with learning difficulties, and what the instructional format might be. Suppose an employee stops work to socialize for a bit but then becomes engrossed in the social topic and continues to socialize for too long a period without getting back to work. The conversational partner – the co-worker – may be the individual in the best position to provide a prompt. But the co-worker may need to be approached and asked to do so, and assisted to identify a suitable reminder sentence or phrase, such as "We'll talk later but we need to get back to work now."

Implications for management and management consulting

Sometimes instead of filling a typical full job position, managers carve out a custom-made job for an employee or intern. For instance, instead of having each insurance office staff person make their own photocopies, a photocopying job is created for Stacy during the afternoon busy period. This arrangement is purposefully designed to increase work efficiency as well as allow Stacy to successfully learn a job, but it may create unintended cultural consequences.

For example, the employees in this office tend to be a bit more social earlier in the day. Someone who comes in late, when everyone is very busy, misses that social opportunity. Keeping in mind that real work efficiency is best achieved when a work group functions as a team, in the context of a healthy workplace culture, it may be best to work with the office staff to identify one or two additional tasks that can take place in the morning, such as distributing the mail, so that Stacy can be present during some of the slower times as well as through the busy period.

If employees in a work group typically are able to make some choices about how to do something or in what order to do several tasks, it is important to consider whether an intern or a supported employee, for example, could be given that same level of choice. Sometimes in an effort to be thorough and specific, the job of an intern or supported employee can be too rigidly "set in stone." This can result in decreased inclusion or the individual being perceived as less capable.

ELEMENT 7: GATHERING PLACES

Are there particular "gathering places" where workers are more likely to talk socially?

A gathering place is some space within a work setting where people tend to collect and engage in more social interactions. As with many elements of a culture, the gathering place may be specifically designated for this purpose by company management, such as a lunch room or employee lounge. Or it may be a place commandeered by employees through a "grassroots" effort, such as the area in front of the mailboxes, the place where wooden pallets are stacked, or one particular diner booth, as is the case at the Greasy Spoon Diner. Workers may gravitate towards these areas during breaks, and also, depending on the culture, at more social times (element #6) when work is slow or workers are between tasks. Knowing about and taking advantage of a gathering place is a sign of belonging. The gathering place becomes a reinforcing and socially important context for interaction.

Assessment

As soon as one gets the "feel" of a worksite – the pattern of busy times, break times, slower times, and so on – it usually becomes fairly obvious where the gathering spots are. Because gathering places are where much socialization occurs, gathering places and patterns of social interaction (element #19) both can be identified together.

One simply can ask workers where they gather. But remember that "gathering place" is our term, not theirs. Asking, "Where are the gathering places?" is asking the workers to turn into anthropologists. Even if they were familiar with the term (i.e. if one is assisting an individual to work at a job in a university department of anthropology), workers may not freely disclose information about a gathering place or places, for any of a variety of reasons. The best way to ask about this and many other elements of a culture is to construct a question that specifically relates to what you are observing and makes sense to the people in the setting. For instance, "Do people usually talk here with the driver for a while when a new shipment pulls up?" What you want to know is whether what you observe over a brief time sample is a customary occurrence (e.g., "I guess you could say that; it breaks things up a little."), something that depends on the person involved (e.g., "Well I always catch up on things with Mike because him and me go way back"), or something rare and impromptu that happened to occur only that time. Some gathering places, such as a lunch wagon, locker area, break room, or water cooler may be connected to food and drink customs or to workplace transitions.

Implications for employment assistance

There are likely to be social customs governing the timing of gatherings and the rituals that take place when workers gather. It may be important to show an individual how to tell when people are free to talk and when they are too busy to talk, how to use the vending machines to get a snack, and how to budget money in order to have cash available for this purpose.

It is also important to help guide a person if needed in structuring social conversations with co-workers. For example, in our casual conversations with new people, we sometimes search for commonalties, points of connection between the two of us that can serve as a basis for further conversation and sharing. The commonalty can be a shared interest, a common place of residence, people known in common, and so on. Some people are better at this type of interaction than others. It may be necessary to facilitate this process on behalf of an employee. For example, an employment specialist can rehearse this type of interaction with an employee in advance, or can learn some things about the co-workers on his or her own and do some "matchmaking" (that is, identify some things a co-worker and the focal employee have in common and engage the two of them in talking about it, then back away).

Implications for management and management consulting

The physical layout of a work space can be designed to facilitate interactions. In an effort to maintain a strong work culture, many businesses provide or enhance an area for use as a comfortable break space.

Make sure that an employee's work routines allow or facilitate access to gathering places. In one situation, a hospital food service department was on two floors, and the elevators commonly were used for brief social conversations. In developing a list of work tasks for an employee with a disability, the supervisor made sure to include at least one function that required traveling between floors, as a good way to make sure the employee got to meet and talk to everyone.

ELEMENT 8: MEALTIMES

Do workers eat lunch (or other meal, depending on the shift) at the same time?

Many of the customs in any culture involve food and drink. Obtaining and preparing food was probably an important group activity in early human societies, and it may partly be for that reason that it feels natural for us to eat together. Workplaces where there is some shared time for eating are stronger than those where people do not eat or eat alone. Eating and drinking are rewarding in themselves, of course, as well as an interruption from the serious concentration that work demands.

Assessment

Mealtimes and their associated customs may be missing, or nearly so, in workplaces where the work day is short or in workplaces where people tend to stagger their eating times or eat while working. Even in these situations, though, two or more people may habitually make sure their meal times coincide, or workers may meet before or after work (element #26). There may be a custom that operates only occasionally, such as eating out at a restaurant on payday. Meal customs also may vary within a setting by subgroup. For example, women and men might eat at different tables.

In addition to the time and place, mealtime customs and interactions should be understood. For example, do most people bring or buy lunch? Do they heat some leftovers in a microwave or keep sandwiches in a refrigerator?

Implications for employment assistance

An employee might need assistance in planning to bring to work some cash for things such as food or drinks, and to prepare for the possibility that the group might be ordering a takeout pizza, collecting contributions for a birthday cake, or stopping someplace after work. If people bring their lunch to work, employment specialists should be alert for the possibility that a student or an individual who previously attended some sort of disability "day program" may be in the habit of carrying their lunch in a childish lunch box. He or she may need some guidance in using an appropriate lunch container. This may require contacting families or residences to enlist their assistance. People also may need assistance eating and drinking properly at the worksite.

It is a good idea to be attentive to any interactions that involve borrowing money or "pitching in" to purchase something, because money customs can be tricky. People are sometimes less direct than they want to be because they feel it is rude, for example, to refuse a request for money or to point out to someone that they didn't pay their fair share. They may become resentful and take it out on the person in some way, or stop inviting the individual to participate. A key role of the employment specialist is to ensure that people feel comfortable being as direct as they need to be, and that they have a way of bringing this type of issue up that meets their needs and also is sufficiently respectful. In addition, one might be able to help the employee learn the fairness rules at a setting, such as not asking for money before returning previously borrowed money, or how to ask others for feedback, such as "Is this enough to contribute?" In some workplace meal areas workers customarily take turns cleaning up. A new worker must learn to take his or her turn.

Implications for management and management consulting

Meal discounts or subsidies at certain hours will facilitate people eating together. Vending machines may be an easy way to ensure the availability of drinks or snacks. Often workers take their cues for expected behavior from the manager, and may interpret a manager's habit of working through lunch as a sign that this behavior is part of "getting ahead." It might be wise to take the time once in a while to model the behavior of sitting down to eat in a relaxed and social atmosphere. There may be a way to provide a specific focus for a group mealtime once in a while, such as a "brown bag" meeting or talk, or to schedule a meeting in the lunch room that starts just as lunch time is ending.

ELEMENT 9: BREAK TIMES
Are there other break times shared by co-workers?
Brief (ten or fifteen minute) breaks are scheduled at specific times and may be announced, such as by a bell, at many workplaces. At other workplaces, workers self-initiate breaks, usually within certain time parameters. They may customarily choose a certain time and place to take their break. As with mealtimes (element #8), social inter-action will be relatively more common during shared breaktimes. The culture of a workplace with an identifiable shared break will, other things being equal, be stronger than one with no opportunity for breaks or with only individual, non-overlapping breaktimes.

Assessment
Shared breaktimes will be absent or negligible as an element of the culture in workplaces with extremely short shifts, in those where individuals work in isolation, and in those with extremely chaotic work demands. Breaktime arrangements and customs generally will be ob-servable in almost any other type of work environment.

Often the basic breaktime schedule and routines at a worksite can be readily observed. But learning the breaktime customs in detail will take time. For instance, how do people know when to begin and end their breaks? What are the food and drink routines? Do workers take turns making coffee or purchasing coffee supplies? If money is collected from individuals for a "coffee run," who collects it? Is change given back to the penny? Can someone owe money? The same level of detail involved in understanding work processes (e.g., in assessing element #3) should be applied to the understanding of breaktime rou-tines.

Implications for employment assistance
Sometimes the cues governing an activity are subtle or indistinct, making it hard for some people to pick up on them. When on their break, for example, workers just may have an internal sense when it is time to return to work, without a detectable prompt or cue. Similarly, a worker just may *have a feeling* that it is probably his or her turn to clean the coffee machine or buy more coffee supplies. Someone with-out the same talent for "just knowing" what to do may be confused, or may get into trouble by failing to engage in the activity at the appro-priate time without realizing why.

Overt, clear cues are always easier to deal with than fuzzy, hard-to-figure-out ones. If an employee is having difficulty catching on to a vague cue, one possible solution is to help the employee to identify or construct a clear cue that serves the same functional purpose. For example an employee might return from break "after two cigarettes." Or an individual could return to work at the same time as a particular co-worker. One also can follow this same principle in helping an employee to clarify or simplify a rule that is too vague or too complex to follow successfully as is.

The identification of a substitute cue or rule must be done correctly. One employment specialist taught an employee with autism to ask co-workers in the break room "Would you like some coffee?" when entering the room for break. But the employee was not taught the more sophisticated aspects of the custom, such as not asking an individual who already is holding a cup of coffee if they would like some coffee. Social rules tend to be complicated. Simplified versions may backfire unless they are developed carefully.

Implications for management and management consulting

Common or shared breaks are more effective in building a healthy workplace culture than individual, isolated breaks. If production demands require that workers take staggered breaks, it may be that this can occur in pairs or small groups, a few at a time. In this type of situation it may be worthwhile to pay attention to who is assigned to take a break with whom. In any event, some provision for food or drink as part of a breaktime – a coffee maker, refrigerator, vending machines, or similar conveniences – will be conducive to a more relaxed and pleasant atmosphere.

If one or more employees have difficulty with the complexity or vagueness of breaktime cues or rules, a clearer rule often can be instituted to cover the situation. For example, if workers take turns cleaning the coffee maker, a rotation list or sign-up sheet will provide an obvious and unambiguous cue. Managers commonly find that solutions like this not only accommodate the needs of employees with disabilities, but are welcomed and appreciated by other employees as well.

ELEMENT 10: ORIENTATION

Does the company provide a formal orientation for new workers?

Orientation refers to a formal process for acquainting a new worker with a company. The orientation period may last anywhere from part of the first day to the first week (Wanous, 1992). The purposes of orientation are to provide some basic information about employment at the company and to decrease the stress of entering a new situation for the employee. A well thought-out orientation is evidence of a commitment on the part of the company to investing in its human resources.

Assessment

A job developer or an applicant will be informed if an orientation is provided by the company. Most orientations consist of group sessions. They may include activities such as viewing a videotape. Sometimes an orientation handbook or handout folder can be made available for review. Attending orientation is not only a part of belonging to the culture in itself, but the material presented in the orientation will to some extent provide clues about other aspects of the culture. Attending orientation thus can be an excellent way to collect workplace culture information. Most companies will not object to allowing a job developer to sit in on an orientation session. Remember that orientation presents only a part of the picture – what you might call the company's official portrayal of itself, or its "party line." Information about the company's self-image is extremely useful, of course, but it is not necessarily the whole story.

Implications for employment assistance

All employees should take advantage of the orientation provided by the company if at all possible. It may be necessary for an employment specialist to help the individual prepare for and understand what will be happening in the orientation – an "orientation to orientation" – or to accompany the individual. The amount of material some companies provide about various benefits packages and company policies can be overwhelming and anxiety-producing.

While some useful information always can be obtained from orientation, one cannot rely on the orientation alone as the vehicle for imparting everything a new employee needs to know. For some employees the orientation will provide an initial exposure to information, but further assistance will be required to go through the material more slowly or in a different format. Many times a human resources office will be glad to schedule an individual follow-up meeting with an employee. This meeting should be in addition to and not instead of the typical orientation, because a group orientation session can result in some social connections with co-workers and because of the message of "differentness" that is given if one doesn't attend.

Often the process of providing employment support for an employee will lead an employment specialist to see some ways in which orientation could be improved. If this is the case, an employment specialist can offer to assist the company in improving or adding various elements. Sometimes the long-term employees designing an orientation have forgotten or have taken for granted something that should be explained to a new employee. This is one situation where being an outsider can be beneficial.

Implications for management and management consulting

Orientation has value for insiders as well as for those entering the organization. It helps reaffirm an organization's values and provides an opportunity to clarify and discuss policies and practices. So putting some thought into developing an orientation program if none exists is usually a worthwhile activity. A good way to begin is:

- Choose employees who have been with the company for six to twelve months (long enough to know what it is one needs to know but not long enough to have forgotten what it's like to be a new employee).
- Ask them to make a list of topics they would recommend be covered in an orientation.

Employees also can be in charge of creating parts of the manual or giving a presentation as part of the orientation. It is essential that the orientation include realistic information and information about "what it's like to work here" judged to be important from the perspective of a worker, not simply from a management point of view. Rothwell and Kazanas (1994) recommend that an orientation cover at least the following topics: (a) safety and health, (b) dress code, (c) attendance, (d) breaks, (e) hours of work, (f) discipline, (g) overtime, (h) parking, (i) appraisal and salary, (j) telephone use, (k) visitors, and (l) vacation time and scheduling.

Employees should be seen as active participants in an orientation program, not merely passive recipients of information. According to Wanous (1992), the best orientation programs have the following characteristics:

- presentation of realistic concrete information every employee needs to know,
- general support and reassurance,
- opportunities to observe people modeling successful coping strategies for anything likely to be stressful, and
- opportunities for new employees to voice their concerns and ask questions.

ELEMENT 11: EMPLOYEE TRAINING

*Are specific arrangements made for employee training,
such as pairing a new worker with a co-worker?*

Arrangements may be relatively informal, such as the manager telling the new employee "You go with Frank." Or it can be a structured training program, possibly consisting of some classroom elements as well as on-the-job training by a co-worker or supervisor. Some companies have staff or a whole department devoted specifically to training.

As it is rare for an employee to enter a job with the complete repertoire of skills required, most companies provide some form of employee training. A national study (Barron, Berger, and Black, 1997) found that in firms employing 100 or more workers, new employees spent an average of about eighty-one hours in training during their first four weeks of employment. This included several different types of training:

- twenty-six hours training by the supervisor or a manager
- twenty-three hours training by a co-worker
- twenty-three hours learning through observation
- eight hours group classroom-style training on the company premises
- two hours group classroom-style training off-site (e.g., at a community college) during work time.

Co-worker and supervisor training do not always occur in neat, preestablished blocks of time. Training may occur in bits and pieces, interspersed with other work activity, as situations arise in the work flow that provide a natural occasion for introducing a new task. There is a method to this madness, because a great deal of useful informal learning (Garrick, 1998) takes place through this training format. A co-worker or supervisor does more than simply teach the worker how to perform various tasks. The individual providing training also will play a key role in helping the individual learn to negotiate social rules, deal with various personalities, and in general fit in with the workplace culture.

One of the key differences between an expert and a novice in any field of endeavor is that the expert knows how to quickly "size up" a situation – that is, discriminate among various contexts by picking up the relevant cues (Federico, 1995). When an expert serves as an on-the-job trainer, he or she models this behavior for the new employee and gradually helps the individual recognize features of the job that indicate context. For instance, a senior receptionist may tell a novice receptionist at a pharmaceutical company to suspend the usual procedure of taking a message when the boss is on another line if the caller identifies him or herself as from the federal Food and Drug Administration, and interrupt the call. An experienced refrigerator technician may show a new technician how to distinguish between frozen coolant coils that indicate a simple buildup of condensation from ones that indicate a serious malfunction by slight differences in the sound of the compressor (Henning, 1998).

Some theorists distinguish between two phases of employee training: *breaking in* and *settling in* (Wanous, 1992). Breaking in involves learning enough of the basics of job performance to begin to be productive. Settling in involves such things as learning the culture, learning the fine points and tangential aspects of the job, and adjusting work to other life domains, such as family, transportation, and leisure. These phases may occur one after the other or overlap with one another, and the same individual or different individuals may take the lead in providing support during each phase.

When one co-worker or supervisor can be identified who plays a major role in employee socialization, we often refer to the individual as a "mentor" (Hagner and DiLeo, 1992). Kennedy (1980) lists several different kinds of workplace mentors, depending on the mix of support functions they perform. An *information mentor* primarily provides concrete job expertise. A *peer mentor* primarily provides affective support and social connections. A *godparent mentor* provides connections and advice that are important for career development. This third type of mentor is usually sought out by an employee, once he or she is acclimated to the job.

Assessment

One readily can find out about formal training programs on an initial informational interview. Such programs may have a syllabus, a manual, or handouts available for review. One also may obtain permission to attend group classroom-style training sessions or to observe an individual being trained.

For informal training, and to learn about the relative importance of formal versus informal training where both occur, it is best to talk with a few workers about how they learned their job. In the case of job training by a co-worker, it is a good idea to find out how the co-worker was selected or how the training relationship got started. If no specific arrangements are made, workers probably will report that they simply were expected to pick up what they need to know through observation and asking, or that one or more co-workers, on their own initiative, gave assistance. Sometimes training related to certain work tasks is handled formally, while training in others is informal.

Implications for employment assistance

Some supported employment programs use the availability of a staff trainer, usually called a job coach, as a selling point in developing jobs for their consumers. This can lead to the employment specialist duplicating or substituting for the co-worker training and mentor function (Lee, Storey, Anderson, Goetz, and Zivolich, 1997; Mank, Cioffi, and Yovanoff, 1997). In companies that do provide some form of employee training, it is better to view the employment specialist as a consultant to or backup for the company's training process.

Viewing the employment specialist role in this way allows for a range of potential options for a training partnership between an employment service and a company. As a training consultant, the employment specialist can pay attention to a variety of factors, such as the work load and schedule of the co-worker trainer and his or her training skill and level of frustration tolerance. Consultation interventions can include modeling or teaching training techniques, filling-in when the co-worker trainer is unavailable, dividing up tasks such that some are taught by the co-worker and others are taught by the employment specialist, advising on documentation of training outcomes, problem-solving, supporting and reinforcing the trainer's efforts, and many others (Hagner and DiLeo, 1993). In a long-term relationship with a company, an employment specialist may be able to assist in the selection of appropriate trainers or mentors.

Employment service personnel also have a role to play as trainers of company personnel such as supervisors and managers in positive supervisory practices. Workforce diversity or disability awareness training to counter myths and misconceptions also may be considered. But be aware that this type of training can put the spotlight on "special" employees and thus backfire. One suggestion is to assist a business to develop a diversity training program and deal with disability as one module in a larger package that also considers gender, ethnicity, age, and other aspects of diversity.

Implications for management and management consulting

According to Rothwell and Kazanas (1994), the two most common barriers to a more systematic use of on-the-job training are a belief that the "school of hard knocks" builds character in an employee, and a perceived lack of time to devote to training. They argue that both positions are faulty and lead to unnecessary turnover, job dissatisfaction, and decreased productivity.

In a systematic training program, selection of a co-worker trainer is made carefully and well in advance of a new employee's start date. Ideally, selection as a trainer should be an indication of substantial expertise and mean that an individual's work is considered exemplary. The personality match of trainer and trainee also should be considered. Hagner and DiLeo (1993) recommended the following guidelines for selecting a co-worker trainer:

- Has the individual worked at the job for at least several months and know the job well?
- Is the individual well-liked by other employees?
- Can the individual be scheduled to work and be freed up from other duties when training will be needed?
- Is the individual interested in accepting the responsibility and, if applicable, in receiving consultation from employment service staff?

Personal "chemistry" is hard to predict. Therefore a planned match between a trainer and trainee must be provisional at first and subject to change. Clear guidelines, such as a learning contract and progress report format, help structure the relationship. Excellent examples of both can be found in Rothwell and Kazanas (1994). Managers must be willing to:

- ensure sufficient coverage of a trainer's usual responsibilities during scheduled training periods so that the individual is not torn between competing responsibilities, and
- support co-worker trainers by providing a source of assistance when a trainer has a question or training problem.

Managers may find that training techniques modeled or taught by employment services staff that may have been originally developed for employees with disabilities are just as applicable to the training of any worker. As a result, training consultation can serve as a catalyst for improvements in a company's training and supervision techniques (Lee, Storey, Anderson, Goetz, and Zivolich, 1997).

ELEMENT 12: INITIATION PRANKS
Do workers typically play some kind of prank on a new employee as a kind of initiation?

Initiation pranks and practical jokes are a typical experience at some work settings. They function as a type of admissions ritual into a group, and perhaps as the work group's way of administering its own brand of parallel co-worker job interview, to assess the new recruit's fit with the culture. The new worker's ability to "take it" can make or break his or her employment. Once an initiation custom is established, it tends to perpetuate itself, because workers may feel that fairness dictates that they do to the next new worker what was done to them. As with all forms of hazing, a worker who speaks out against the custom risks ostracism or retaliation.

Assessment

Pranks will form part of the underground culture of a workplace, not generally visible to or sanctioned by management. An example of an initiation prank would be hiding from a new employee the uniform, keys, or other item that was recently issued to him or her (element #14) along with a warning about being responsible. As another example, a new employee at one rural feed store can expect to open his or her lunch box on the first day and find a dead mouse inside. Another sort of more passive type of prank is to allow a new employee to make a beginner's mistake without intervening to stop it or alerting the employee as to what is about to happen. Henning (1998) observed that refrigeration technicians are considered "baptized" into the group when on one for their first repair attempts they make the mistake of releasing a valve too quickly and are sprayed with pressurized refrigerant.

If it is possible to get a couple of employees to talk about their first day or two at work, initiation stories may surface. Occasionally one may be lucky (or unlucky) enough to be present on someone's first day on the job and observe a prank in action. But not observing a prank nor hearing an initiation story cannot be taken as proof that none exists. It may be that this aspect of the culture is hidden from outsiders.

Implications for employment assistance

In the event that one comes to know about an initiation prank ahead of time, it is a good idea to inform the employee what to expect. Same employment services include being present with the employee on his or her first day or two of work. If so, "hanging back" and letting natural interactions take place, while remaining attentive and available, allows the initiation prank to occur. It also allows the employment specialist several options regarding how and when to best support the individual in getting through it.

If the individual will be paired with a co-worker trainer or mentor (element #11) but you will not be present, you might schedule a meeting with the co-worker and employee before the first day to review the job, the individual's learning style or support needs, and what the first day will be like. It is a good idea to directly ask the co-worker at that point if a new person in a situation like this would be teased or have a prank played on him or her. This will help communicate to the co-worker that guiding the person through the experience is a valid part of his or her role. (How the co-worker responds to the question is of secondary importance.)

If you will not be present and it is unknown what degree of support the individual may receive if and when they are subjected to a prank, be sure to meet the employee after work or talk soon after by phone and ask the individual to relate what happened at work. This provides an opportunity to discuss any incidents that were problematic for the individual.

Implications for management and management consulting

Harmless initiation pranks can be a symptom of a healthy, albeit "underground" culture. In any event, a direct head-on intervention probably never will eradicate the custom.

It may be worthwhile to investigate whether workers feel a sense of powerlessness or have some other complaint that is behind the custom. If so, it may be something that can be addressed in an open way. Giving co-workers a sense that they have some input into new employee selection, for instance by arranging for the top candidates to meet a few of their prospective co-workers and then genuinely listening to the workers' advice on the decision, will counteract the need for workers to feel that they have to conduct their own surreptitious job interview. Sometimes what is expressed through humor and joking is what people feel cannot be brought into the open (Dwyer, 1991).

Pranks vary in their degree of meanness. When performed in an essentially friendly and humorous manner, they are not only harmless but a positive sign of welcome and acceptance. At the other end of the spectrum, pranks can degenerate into victimization, humiliation, and harassment. Some express prejudice and negative attitudes towards diversity. Particularly in relation to employees who are members of groups that have historically been subject to unequal treatment, it is important to pay attention to the individual's reaction and demeanor. Becoming withdrawn or irritable is sometimes a warning sign of harassment. Managers need to attend to such warning signs immediately, as well, of course, to any reported complaint of unacceptable behavior.

ELEMENT 13: SPECIAL TERMS AND JARGON

Are there special terms or language used by the workers?

Language differences are perhaps the most obvious distinguishing features of different cultures. A workplace is likely to have some distinctive terms or language usage that identify the users as members. As with many elements of workplace culture, special terms also may convey workplace humor, such as the nickname "roach coach" for a lunch van. At my current workplace, I learned on my first day that a popular place to purchase an inexpensive lunch is called the "dump" because it's initials are DMP.

Many occupations and fields of work have names for specialized materials, equipment, and work procedures, unique to that particular field. They may be unusual words or words used with a different meaning than in ordinary language. Some restaurants, for example, distinguish between rags used for wiping eating surfaces and rags for cleaning floors, appliances, or other purposes by referring to the former as "bar towels." Special terms also function as a type of shorthand, or code, that speeds up communication among workers. As new employees receive training, they are taught the shorthand expressions, acronyms, nicknames, and special jargon that go hand-in-hand with learning the work operations and becoming familiar with the facility. The refrigerator technicians studied by Henning (1998), for example, were taught that the boss "doesn't like to see your head float." This expression meant that the boss wanted technicians to set the refrigerant pressure slightly higher than the level recommended in the service manual.

Assessment

Observation of interactions will begin to identify special terms in common use at a workplace. Especially valuable, if the opportunity presents itself, is observing and listening in on the training of a new worker by a co-worker or supervisor. If the presence of an additional person would be too disruptive, it may be possible to have a worker audiotape an on-the-job training session, or to debrief the trainer at break or after work about his or her training process. A great deal can be learned by asking workers to describe their work and explain what objects in the environment are called and what they are for, and then listening to the terms that are used. Special terms and language also may be picked up by attending orientation, or may appear in written documents such as procedure manuals or memos.

Implications for employment assistance

Whenever possible, an experienced co-worker should be assigned as the primary instructor responsible for helping a new employee learn the job, rather than the employment specialist. An important reason for this recommendation is that, along with the work methods and operations imparted during training, co-workers help a new worker become familiar with the special terms and jargon they use to talk about their work and they way they communicate with one another.

But this does not mean that an employment specialist should be uninvolved in training. If some workplace terms are introduced that a worker needs assistance to remember or keep straight, an employment specialist may assist in partnership with the co-worker trainer by going over difficult terms later in a shift or outside of work. In that way, the employment specialist is seen as backing-up or aiding the co-worker trainer, rather than taking the lead.

In going about consulting with and backing-up worksite personnel, employment specialists should try to be aware of the special terms and jargon they have learned from working in the disability field that are not generally helpful or meaningful in the context of a community job. For example, we use the special term "gathering place" as a way of helping us understand workplace cultures. It is not that there is something wrong with any particular terms, acronyms, or usage of language, only with using them in the wrong context. In reporting on progress to funding agencies, brainstorming issues with other employment specialists, and similar contexts, it might save time to refer to "ADHD" or "Axis II," but work-setting personnel outside the disability field will be confused or possibly even put off by these terms.

Implications for management and management consulting

Sometimes a difficulty remembering the names of equipment and other items is easily accommodated for by labeling the items whose names need to be learned. In analyzing a workplace, supported employment and other employment service staff are trained to be attentive to special terms and their meaning. An entire department or organization might benefit from a compilation of these into a list or glossary of terms. One Gap clothing store was impressed by a list of "Gap Terms" developed to assist a new worker with a disability, and incorporated the list as part of its regular orientation materials for all new employees (Hagner and Faris, 1994).

ELEMENT 14: ITEMS ISSUED TO EMPLOYEES

Are any items issued to new employees
(e.g., locker, key, uniform, tools)?

Although their primary purpose is utilitarian, possession of an item such as a key, ID badge, or set of tools that typically is distributed to a worker comes to have a secondary purpose as well. It identifies the bearer as a full-fledged member of the work group, both to others and also to the individual himself or herself. The item then functions as a symbol of membership. Sometimes an individual's pride in the job is expressed and felt as pride in the uniform, the keys, or the tool kit.

Assessment

The pagers worn by the waitresses at the Greasy Spoon Diner so they can be beeped when an order is "up" are an example of a personal item distributed by the employer. ID cards or badges are another common example. These items are usually easy to identify or ask about during the job development or job application phase.

Implications for employment assistance

When a job is designed to meet an individual's unique needs, such as to accommodate for a disability, pay attention to the possibility that some items may function as membership symbols and thus will need to be designed into the job. For instance, suppose only one worker at a company takes public transportation, and in order to conform to the bus schedule this worker is allowed to arrive at work twenty minutes later than the usual starting time and work twenty minutes longer in the afternoon. The business might reason that there would be no possibility of this individual being the first one into the building, so no key to the building is issued. An item also may be withheld from an employee out of safety concerns. For example, there might be a fear that the employee might lose or break something, compromise security by complying with a request to lend the key to some unauthorized person, use a tool in a hazardous manner, and so on.

To the extent possible, employment specialists should advocate for an employee to have access to any items identified as membership symbols. Usually a sound case can be made for this. For example, there is always a possibility that bad weather might prevent cars from getting to work before the bus, and thus the individual would need a key. If something is important enough for other people to have, a compelling argument should be made for everyone to have it.

Rather than deny an item due to safety concerns, it is up to the employment specialist to plan with the employer and the employee to ensure that the item is cared for properly and used safely. This may require employee training, an assistive device such as a key case, or coordination with those providing assistance at an individual's home.

If a key, tool, or other item typically is given to a worker not when they first enter the job but later, at the end of a probationary or training period, the item will function as a status indicator. Possession of the item will indicate that it has been earned. This can be a natural incentive for a worker to complete his or her probationary period satisfactorily. It can be linked to reaching a certain production quota or quality standard. The item should be given to the employee by the appropriate company personnel, not by employment service staff.

Implications for management and management consulting

In a situation in which an item is necessary for all but one or two positions within a work group, it may be advisable to look at whether changes can be made in work schedules (element #5), in access to the workplace (elements #7 and 15), or in whether more joint tasks can be introduced (element #2) so that the item needs to be issued to the whole group. Whenever one subgroup can be distinguished from another in some easily recognized way (for example, some workers wear hard hats and others don't), there is a strong possibility that cliques will form based on the difference. In a workplace where this type of differentiation is something unavoidable, or something desirable, it might be best to consider each clique separately for the purposes of analyzing the workplace culture.

ELEMENT 15: SHARED EQUIPMENT
Is there any equipment that workers share the use of?

Using things in common helps create a sense of community. The name of the landscaped area in the center of many New England towns – the commons – typifies the way in which a community can come to center around what is used in common. In colonial times, the commons was a grassy area set aside for use in common for grazing animals. The shared experience of using something in common, as well as the necessity to engage in interactions related to negotiating the sharing, such as asking someone, "Are you going to be using that much longer?", help shape the culture of a workplace.

Assessment

Common examples of shared equipment are the fax machine and copy machine in an office or the washing station in a factory. Job analyses of several positions will uncover tasks that share equipment. Often a visual inspection of a work area can identify items that are either too expensive to purchase many of, or are relatively fixed at the setting, such as equipment tied to a water line or a telephone/modem port. These pieces of equipment will tend to have shared use.

Implications for employment assistance

It is a good idea to identify one or two pieces of shared equipment during an initial job analysis visit to a company, and design a proposal to the company that builds in the use of the shared equipment. For instance, a clerical assistant job might be designed to include the task of photocopying. Existing jobs also can be enriched or enlarged in a direction that emphasizes greater use of shared equipment. For example, a mail sorter position might be enlarged to also include distribution of incoming faxes.

When equipment is shared, it is important that an employee learn the specific rules for sharing it with other employees. For example, one department might have priority over others in the use of a piece of equipment, or there may be a schedule dictating the use. If there are no formal rules, an informal "pecking order" or rules of politeness, such as noticing when someone is in a hurry and offering, "Why don't you go ahead," may govern the interactions related to sharing. These interactions represent opportunities for an employee to participate in the give-and-take of workplace support, for other employees to learn to communicate better with the employee, and for interactions to spill over into social comments.

Implications for management and management consulting

Many people in our society feel that there is not as strong a sense of community in our neighborhoods and towns as there once was. Part of this is due to the simple fact that many of us have more material wealth than our predecessors and can afford to privately and separately own more of the things we use. This is convenient, but it also has the unfortunate side-effect of isolating us more from one another. Similarly, the use of shared equipment is not always the most convenient workplace design. Sometimes it is demonstrably less efficient from a purely time-and-motion-study perspective. Some time may be lost in waiting for someone else to finish or getting to the equipment from across the room.

But if one of our goals is to maintain a healthy, productive culture, it may be good company policy for several people to share a fax machine, for example, even though the company has ample resources to put one at each work station. Or, if opportunities for sharing are decreased in one area, care should be taken that they are increased in some other area. In the long run, healthier work cultures are the ones that are truly more efficient.

Minor annoyances and conflicts related to using shared equipment are to be expected, as are opportunities for teamwork and problem-solving. Suggesting to a work group that it come up with a procedure everyone is comfortable with empowers the group to come up with its own solution. A sign-in sheet or a posted schedule are the most common procedures used to structure the demand for something people need to share.

In some situations, job analysis may turn up instances of shared use that are indeed unproductive. For instance, highly skilled and highly paid staff should not spend inordinate amounts of time waiting for one another to finish photocopying. The purchase of a second copier is one solution, but not necessarily the most cost-effective. There may be an opportunity to restructure jobs and create a new position devoted solely to photocopying. This new position will use time efficiently and will have task intersections built in, as various employees refer their copy jobs to the employee. Thus, it will add to the culture in a way that purchasing a second photocopier cannot.

ELEMENT 16: DRESS AND APPEARANCE
Is there a particular code of dress or appearance for employees?

Dress indicates one's degree of affiliation with a particular group or setting. It also expresses to some extent the values of a group (Rafaeli and Pratt, 1993). For example, hospital "scrub" dress promotes an image of cleanliness. Sometimes dress differs among various subcultures or cliques within an organization. As with many elements of culture, there is a band of acceptability regarding dress and appearance in a workplace. Being overdressed or underdressed refers to a manner of dress that is above or below this band. Individual variations are allowed and even may be highly valued, but only if they are scrupulously kept within the prescribed band of acceptability.

Assessment

Basic dress and appearance "themes" are relatively easy to observe, making this element one that can be considered during the investigation or job development phase. But there may be nuances that are not apparent at first. For example, there may be a custom of "dress down Fridays" when people can be more casual than during the rest of the week. Some dress customs are far less frequent. Many places uphold the tradition of wearing something green on St. Patrick's Day, and some workplaces occasionally may have some sort of special dress custom like "wear purple day," governed by its own unique rules.

Implications for employment assistance

Obtaining appropriate clothing and personal appearance supplies involves spending money. So it may be important to assist an employee and anyone else involved in budgeting to identify an appropriate amount to invest in these articles out of take-home pay. Sometimes an employee will need direct assistance in shopping and picking clothing out. Once in a while, if he or she is asked, a co-worker might be interested in accompanying an employee on a shopping expedition and helping select suitable clothing.

If cleanliness or hygiene is an issue, avoid making assumptions about what the problem might be. Find out, through either detailed questioning or a home visit. In one situation an employee had a persistent body odor problem, despite showering daily with soap and hot water, drying off with a clean towel, wearing deodorant, and putting on clean clothes. A home visit identified that the individual brought home clean laundered clothing and placed them on top of a pile of very dirty laundry, so that the clean clothes picked up the odor. Once identified, the problem could be resolved.

As with every element, workplace cultures differ immensely in their standards and customs of hygiene and grooming. Rather than dictating standards to others, look for appropriate job matches.

For an employment specialist, identifying workplace customs is a mandatory task. But intervening to facilitate inclusion depends on the culture. Some of the customs identified may relate to introducing and orienting a new employee to the culture. Directly intervening may subvert these and do more harm than good. One needs to judge the extent to which typical socialization mechanisms are likely to be effective. For example, can the employee pick up on the kinds of hints that are being given about proper dress and appearance? If not, then intervention is called for. But, depending again on the culture, it might be best for employment specialist intervention to be focused on the person being given hints (the receptive side of the communication), or on the person or people doing the hinting (the expressive side of the communication). Thus there are always two potential "clients" for an employment specialist: the employee and the employer.

Implications for management and management consulting

Our culture has a rule that says "don't be too blunt." In other words, we often give subtle hints – a certain "look," clearing the throat, and so on – instead of coming right out and saying what we mean, in order to not be perceived as rude or overbearing. For instance, during an orientation session an employee with a learning disability yawned loudly. The instructor turned to her and asked, "Did you have a late night last night?" But not all employees can decode subtle hints. This employee answered "No, I went to bed early," unaware that she had been given a subtle hint.

This same type of subtlety often is used to comment on dress, grooming, and hygiene problems. If there are expectations for dress, appearance, and hygiene in the workplace, a supervisor must be able to give clear feedback in this area as in any other area that affects job performance. Being overly subtle actually can be more rude than being blunt, because it denies the individual the opportunity to learn what to do differently the next time.

It is helpful to have a written personnel policy statement about dress and appearance, to explain the expectations to employees as part of their initial orientation (element #10), and to refer to them as situations arise. If needed, employment consultants can assist in developing such a policy. Being clear and direct with feedback about dress and appearance may be not only required, but appreciated.

ELEMENT 17: NAME DISPLAY

Are workers' names displayed, such as on mailboxes, doors, or a posted schedule?

If worker names are visible or evident within the setting, the names will constitute a sort of registry of group membership, in addition to serving whatever utilitarian purpose is involved. A missing name indicates nonmembership in the work group.

Assessment

Observation can determine whether there are mail slots, names on lockers, a call-in list by the managers's phone, or some other display of employee's names that is observable by company personnel. The listing of employee names in personnel or other files, hidden from view, should not be considered part of this element, because there is no display of the names. However, the telephone system and e-mail lists should be included. For example, employees may have telephone extensions reachable through a receptionist or through an automatic system such as entering the first three digits of the individual's last name. Most types of name display will be relatively easy to assess as long as one has access to the work area. This element can be determined in phase one, prior to accepting or beginning a job.

Implications for employment assistance

To maximize inclusion in the culture, arrange for an employee to obtain a mail slot or to be listed on the "sub list" to be called if the department is short-staffed, or whatever particular customs of this kind may apply to the worksite. This will help ensure that the employee is viewed as a full member and will lead to increased interactions and supports. And conversely, exclusion from the name list or display will have negative consequences.

One of the worst things that can happen to employment specialists is for *their* name, not the employees name, to be on a call-in list or other name display. This shows that the employer's primary relationship is not with the employee but with a support person or agency. The best way to avoid this is by going about job development in a more employee-centered way (Hagner and DiLeo, 1993). The aim of a job developer is to facilitate a relationship between employer and employee. When the employer's primary relationship is with agency staff, support services have been oversold. That is, instead of being accommodations or supports to help the employer and employee do business together more successfully, agency services have become the primary commodity that has been purchased. If such an outcome already has occurred, substantial, emergency-level steps need to be taken if the employee is to become included in the workplace culture.

Implications for management and management consulting

As with items issued to employees (element # 14), sometimes an individual's name will be left out of a displayed list or area for a plausible reason. For example, a job coach or other support person's name may be on the supervisor's "on call" sheet instead of the employee's name because it is that person who would drive the employee to work when called in as a substitute. Even though the rationale makes sense, a better approach would be to include the employee as the central agent. For example, the support person can arrange call forwarding from the employee's phone number to his or her number. Or the individual can be provided with a way to page the support person immediately upon getting a call from the supervisor.

When an individual is working on a temporary or trainee status, such as an internship, and is not a true employee, it still may be possible to arrange for the individual to use a telephone extension, mail slot, or other system used by employees, as part of the effort to make the experience realistic. If the setting is primarily providing a time-limited work experience for an individual in a particular type of business or setting who then will make use of it in some other more permanent job, it may be legitimate to be satisfied with less-than-complete inclusion in the culture of the training site.

If this is the case – and it is important that all parties be clear about the purpose from the start – the company's focus in a training or work experience situation is properly on:
- developing employee skills that transfer to other settings,
- developing good general work and work-related habits and behaviors,
- compiling a fair and detailed evaluation of an individual's strengths and weaknesses at the end of the work experience period or at predetermined intervals,
- providing a letter of reference that the individual can use in his or her job search, and
- making available to the trainee any contacts, information, or leads company personnel may be able to provide through their personal networking and familiarity with the industry or work field. Inclusion in the culture still should be sought in as many areas as possible, because the meaning of the experience depends on its degree of realism.

ELEMENT 18: WORK SPACE PERSONALIZATION

*Do workers personalize their work space
with posters, coffee mugs, or other articles?*

Workers add personal touches to their work space in different ways and for different reasons. Work space personalization evidences a certain level of commitment of workers to their jobs. Employees who view themselves as just "passing through" on the way to something else or as "just another cog in the wheel" have little incentive to add personal touches. Personalization contributes to job satisfaction and, because it reflects an employee's outside interests, can become a topic of social conversation. Personal touches also show that an employer encourages some sense of employee ownership and individualization of personal work space.

Assessment

Personalization can be found in the work areas of offices, factories, and many other kinds of work settings. Common examples are coffee mugs; posters on the wall; house plants; quotes, sayings, or cartoons; and family photographs. Personal items are observed fairly easily during the job search phase if you can see individual work stations. These items come in handy as conversation "ice breakers" during a job analysis or job shadowing visit. In addition to individual work stations, personal items may be observed in a coat room or locker room and in a break room or area. If possible, as part of this assessment, note the degree to which workers feel territorial about their personal work space.

Implications for employment assistance

Sometimes employment assistance can become compartmentalized to the extent that an employment specialist does not learn much about an individual outside of the job. Providing assistance regarding how to personalize work space may be a good opportunity to find out about the person in a wider context. One can make suggestions or even accompany an individual on a shopping expedition to purchase something for the office that will express who he or she is to others. This role has some similarities with the role of an image consultant, such as a politician might hire to help think of ways to project a desired image. In addition to responding to inquiries about their own personal items, workers also can be assisted to learn the skill of asking a co-worker about their personal items.

Some individuals with disabilities use assistive technology at their work station. Care should be taken that this technology not seem forbidding or mysterious to others in the work setting. One strategy might be to personalize the technology in some way. One employee, for example, who used a pointer attached to a hat for typing, selected his favorite baseball team hat for this purpose. During baseball season co-workers stopping by to deliver or pick up work often remark on how the team is doing.

Employment specialists also should be sensitive to any effect that work station modifications might have on the work spaces of nearby workers. For instance, widening an aisle to accommodate a wheelchair may shrink someone else's work space and potentially cause resentment. It may be possible to redesign the solution in a way that avoids this outcome, bring the affected workers in as partners in developing the accommodation so they feel some ownership over it, or, if nothing else, to note and plan to deal with any resentment.

Implications for management and management consulting

Within limits set by safety requirements and corporate policy (e.g., a prohibition on items that might be interpreted as demeaning or discriminatory towards other employees), a healthier workplace culture is achieved if employees are allowed some freedom to personalize their work space. This can go beyond passive allowance and include positive recognition and valuing of personal items, such as holding a contest for the "weirdest coffee mug."

ELEMENT 19: SOCIAL INTERACTIONS

Do employees sometimes talk socially during work time?
Social interactions with co-workers and supervisors, such as greetings, joking, and teasing; brief comments that spill over from work related interactions; and "small talk" of various kinds – e.g., personal compliments, inquiries about personal life – are part of the fabric of the work day for most employees. Whether during a slow point in the work schedule (element #6) or slipped into the ongoing stream of work activity, these social interactions develop and shape workplace relationships. Through social interactions, the culture is formed, expressed, and passed along.

Assessment
Included in this element are primarily those interactions that occur during work time itself. Breaktime and lunchtime interactions are covered in elements #8 and #9, although not every worksite has a clear dividing line.

Social interactions include greetings and small-talk, such as asking "How was your weekend?" on Monday and "What are you going to do this weekend?" on Friday. Other social interactions spill over from work-related interactions. For example, one waitress called in the following order to the cook: "I need a quiche and a back massage." The first part was work-related; the second part was a social spill-over. Unexpected occurrences and disruptions of a normal routine are other occasions for social interaction.

As with the example above, many social interactions at work involve joking and teasing. Although most of us participate in it, analyzing humor and the conversational rules we are following when we are being funny is surprisingly difficult. There are various theories about what humor is. According to one theory, workplace messages are expressed as jokes when for some reason they cannot be communicated directly (Dwyer, 1991).

Sometimes recurring conversational themes or topics can be identified. Some workers carry on lengthy conversations on all sorts of topics throughout a work shift, pausing occasionally for a "work break."

Storytelling about workplace events and characters is a form of social interaction that has particularly rich cultural meaning. For example, in Henning's (1998) participant observation study he found that the refrigeration service technicians he studied told stories about mistakes on the job to newcomers as a way of easing their fears and teaching them best practices. When listening to a story, the following questions, adapted from Hansen and Kahnweiler (1993), can assist in the interpretation of cultural meaning.

(1) What do people take credit for? To what do they attribute success or failure?

(2) What are conflicts over and how are conflicts resolved?

(3) What member traits are viewed as positive and negative?

(4) Which people are perceived as "us" and which as "them"?

Social interactions can be well understood only through prolonged exposure to a setting. To some extent, gathering places (element #7), other occasions for social interaction (element #6), and the basic or most common patterns of social interaction all can be identified together. Then, in order to obtain a more in-depth understanding, one can concentrate one's observations on the times and places identified as most frequently associated with social interactions.

Implications for employment assistance

Employment assistance should be provided as much as possible in a way that does not establish a staff person as the social interaction partner for an employee. In other words, on-site support at the workplace must allow some distance and not be in the form of "hovering" over or next to an employee whenever it is not absolutely necessary to do so. As long as a staff member is perceived as accompanying the individual, a co-worker is likely to assume that the interaction partner role is "taken."

Similarly, don't interpret for people or interfere in interactions unless it is absolutely necessary. (If someone needs help understanding an individual, consider giving people that assistance either ahead of time or later on as a form of debriefing, instead of interrupting the interaction).

Make sure that the individual is able to participate in customs related to initiating and responding to social interactions. This can be accomplished through the individual himself or herself picking up this information or being a "social person" to begin with, through co-worker assistance or through the direct assistance of the employment specialist. Learning co-worker names and smiling and making eye contact are a good starting point.

To assist an employee to partake in workplace humor, it is helpful to remember two important rules of teasing and joking: (1) You have to know when to stop; and (2) The rule of reciprocity, as one worker put it, "If you dish it out, you better be ready to take it." A worker may benefit from having these rules and the consequences of ignoring them pointed out.

Socializing while working is particularly complex. Often one or the other is done poorly. Sometimes there is no salient cue for when to stop and the interaction itself is rewarding in the short run, so an employee does not stop socializing soon enough. An effective intervention is simply to ask a co-worker if he or she would give the employee a reminder at the correct point. A respectful and empowering way to do this is to ask the employee what reminder he or she would recommend; in other words, construct a prompt sentence such as "We've talked enough, let's get back to work" in collaboration with the employee and his or her co-worker and potential interaction partner.

Implications for management and management consulting

Because social and work-related interactions continually are being intermingled at a work setting, it is common to find some work information being communicated through a process called the "grapevine" or the "rumor mill." When this type of communication is excessive, it can lead to misinformation, suspicion, and unhealthy clique formation. Cliques can divide workers into camps and lead to conflict. You cannot shut down the "grapevine," but a manager can keep aware of what is being communicated by being part of the informal socializing network. Kennedy (1980) recommends that managers insert their own information when necessary into the grapevine.

Rumors can be an indication that there are not enough avenues for direct communication among the members of a work group and between workers and managers. Sometimes a preponderance of rumors indicates that too little information is being relayed by management, resulting in organizational "blind spots" and "facades" (Galpin, 1995). Rumors then circulate to fill this vacuum. Clear messages are not sufficient. Messages must be communicated, repeatedly and consistently, through several different channels or media (e.g., company newsletter, staff meeting, and memorandum).

ELEMENT 20: GROUP CUSTOMS

Are there particular social customs workers follow, such as taking turns making coffee?

Group customs are interactions that several workers engage in together and that have shared meaning to them. Company-sponsored group customs are covered in element #25. Dress-related customs are covered in element #16. The special case of celebrations is covered in element #24. Many other additional types of group customs may emerge at a work setting. Participating in these customs may be an essential part of belonging to the culture.

Assessment

Group customs are ascertained by a combination of questioning and relatively long-term exposure to the work setting. Participating in a football game "pool," playing catch with a dishrag while waiting for the dishroom conveyor to start up, contributing to a coffee fund and taking turns making coffee, and playing poker during lunch are examples of group customs. Some customs may be harder to detect and understand than others. These include customs like a Superbowl Pool that are infrequent, and those engaged in more surreptitiously, like snacking on food from the supply room. Often one can observe not the custom itself but people referring to or talking about it. Those observations may provide clues regarding how to find out more.

Implications for employment assistance

A co-worker mentor (element #11) or other co-worker may step forward and introduce the individual to significant workplace customs or workers may expect to be asked about it by the new worker. In the latter situation, co-workers may assume that an individual does not want to participate, when actually the individual may be waiting to be invited or unsure of what to do. Co-workers might take the initiative and invite the employee if they are prompted to do so and helped to interpret the new worker's behavior correctly.

As much care should be taken ensuring that the individual learns the rules for following group customs as is taken ensuring that the individual learns his or her job tasks. For instance, one employment specialist found that the workers at a university copy center always played poker during lunch break. She met each day after work with the new worker she was assisting and taught him to play poker, until he was proficient enough to join in.

Sometimes one can identify a co-worker who takes on the role of social coordinator at a worksite. A social coordinator is the person who makes suggestions, gets people involved, and plans events. If an individual like this is identified, every effort should be made to enlist the individual as an ally in breaking down social barriers and assisting an employee who is having some difficulty being included.

The response of an employment service can become extremely tricky when workplace customs are unauthorized (e.g., stealing food; dealing drugs). Usually employment service staff cannot be in the position of even passively sanctioning overt violations or crimes, let alone teaching the individual to participate. Yet "telling on" the workers can prompt retaliation towards the employee one is supporting. If co-workers are teaching an unauthorized custom and one can plausibly deny knowing about it, there are still serious difficulties. Following unauthorized customs without getting caught may involve complex rules and fine discriminations that an employee may not be able to pull off. Situations may arise in which an employee may be "set up" or scapegoated by co-workers. And finally, workers themselves may be offended by or uncomfortable with the custom. Each situation needs to be carefully dissected. An employment specialist should call upon his or her own job supports when needed, from a supervisor or trusted peer.

Implications for management and management consulting

Most customs are either harmless or are a positive force cementing workplace relationships and improving morale. But sometimes work groups or cliques develop customs that are unauthorized or are against company policy. These may become evident only when an individual is not able to engage in the custom skillfully enough to avoid getting caught. If possible, these issues should be investigated and dealt with as issues for the whole department or work group, rather than through "scapegoating" one employee. Efforts to build and reinforce positive group customs help create replacements for a custom that cannot be allowed to continue.

ELEMENT 21. STAFF MEETINGS

Are there staff or employee meetings?

Get-togethers tend to reinforce the common purpose and vision of a work group and increase the arena for shared understandings among workers. While primarily work-related in purpose, meetings are also occasions for informal social interaction. This element also should include union meetings, if these are held on site at a company.

Assessment

Information about staff or employee meetings can be obtained from a supervisor or department head. Sometimes it is possible to see meeting notices posted on a bulletin board or announced in some other way. For an in-depth understanding, just knowing when and where meetings are held is inadequate. It is best to attend a meeting and observe the informal rules of participation in these meetings. For example, there may be a "pecking order" regarding who talks first.

If it is not possible to sit in on a meeting, conversations with employees may reveal some of the needed details. Often the best informants, for this as well as other elements of culture, are fairly recent employees (e.g., new within the past three to six months) because they can remember back when, as new employees, they were more conscious of the details related to fitting in.

Implications for employment assistance

Make sure an employee's work schedule and job design permit participation in company meetings whenever possible. Usually, positive participation enhances an employee's image. Employees can be given some suggestions or prompting regarding participation. But it is important to ensure and verify that the informal rules of participation are followed. For example, at some worksites it is considered prudent to attend several meetings quietly before beginning to interject one's own views. And some workers may need to be specifically taught social rules that we tend to take for granted, such as being quiet when someone else is speaking.

Implications for management and management consulting

The social connection function of work group meetings serves important management goals, in addition to its value for disseminating information, discussing plans, and so on. If a department or work section spans two or more different locations (3rd floor and 4th floor, or uptown and downtown), it may be more efficient to hold a joint meeting. But there also should be some occasion for just those workers at an individual site to meet together.

Food and drink lend a more relaxed and informal atmosphere to a gathering, and should be a standard feature of staff meetings. Meetings are most productive when participants feel that they are actively participating. Practices such as taking a few minutes at the start of the meeting to collect any agenda items from the group, or providing a sign-up board ahead of time for this purpose, will send the right message. The assignment of rotating facilitators or note-takers further enhances participant ownership of the meeting.

ELEMENT 22: PERFORMANCE REVIEW

Is worker job performance formally reviewed by the supervisor?

All supervisors assess and evaluate worker performance. Most work settings have some sort of formal mechanism in place to guide and structure the assessment. A survey by Locher (1988) reported that 94% of companies had formal appraisal programs. Appraisal formats and types varied widely:

- 57% had rating scales
- 21% used narrative descriptions
- 18% used management-by-objectives-type evaluation systems
- 4% used a variety of other formats

Assessment

Company management or a human resource office can provide a copy of whatever formal appraisal forms or policies are in use at a company. It is also a good idea to ask the supervisor of a work area how he or she evaluates performance, because some have their own individual interpretations of or additions to the typical procedure. In the case of a company with only an informal, unwritten evaluation system, one can ask the supervisor how he or she evaluates performance and gives feedback to subordinates.

Implications for employment assistance

Employment service agencies have mechanisms of their own for evaluating work behavior, sometimes dictated by funding source requirements. It may be tempting for agency personnel to ask a company supervisor to complete the agency's checklist or evaluation form for the employee they are supporting. However, it is important that a supervisor use his or her familiar and typical method, not yours, for evaluating an employee. Asking an employer to complete a special evaluation for one employee communicates the wrong message. Sometimes the employer has no formal system, or the one he or she has is not very useful and you know a better one. Then the best strategy is to ask if the current system is working or could use improvement. If so, offer to help develop an effective appraisal program for the whole company or department.

Research on performance evaluation has found that two types of employee "impression management" strategies are associated with higher performance ratings from supervisors (Wayne and Liden, 1995). Employment staff can teach employees these strategies. The first type are *self-presentation* strategies: (a) occasionally reporting to one's supervisor on successful accomplishments, (b) working especially hard on tasks that are more important or visible to the supervisor, and (c) interacting in a polite and friendly manner. The second type are *other-enhancement* strategies: (a) doing small personal favors like bringing coffee to the supervisor, (b) offering personal compliments to the supervisor, (c) praising the supervisor for his or her accomplishments, and (d) taking an interest in the supervisor's personal life. One caution that especially applies to the self-enhancement strategies is that they are effective only in small, subtle, and infrequent doses. If one overdoes it, they will backfire.

Sometimes supervision may involve disciplining a worker or responding to infractions of workplace rules. This can be handled best by asking the employer to sit down with the employee and explain what is expected. It should always be the supervisor or manager who explains the rules to the employee. Clear disciplinary steps also should be explained and enforced.

When an employee is progressing in his or her skills and work behaviors, but at a slower rate than a manager is used to, he or she may benefit from learning to use and interpret a chart that measures a behavior and tracks its increase or decrease over time. For example, swearing at co-workers may be unacceptable, and it may be that Ruth will swear at co-workers for some time to come, but at a slowly decreasing rate. It is unlikely that an employer's existing evaluation system can track small differences in performance with precision. But this sort of tracking may allow a manager to see progress and judge the effectiveness of his or her supervision. It is critical that managers be able to make such judgments. The meaning of performance, whether it is improving or not, and the relationship between supervisory input and change in performance (Sandelands, Glynn, and Larson, 1991) are much more important to a supervisor than the level of performance at one point in time. This needs not conflict with the practice of using the company's evaluation. An addendum to the evaluation that includes a performance chart can be a reasonable modification of a usual procedure to accomplish a specific purpose.

Employment service staff have a wealth of expertise related to employee supervision, coaching, and performance development that company supervisors and managers can benefit from. For instance, from their involvement and consultation with supported employment staff, managers can become more aware of the importance of giving frequent positive feedback and reinforcement to their employees, as opposed to commenting only when things go wrong (Lee, Storey, Anderson, Goetz, and Zivolich, 1997).

Implications for management and management consulting

Some managers have a tendency to want to be "too nice" and not mention problems that arise in supervising or managing an employee who is new to the workforce. There may be a tendency to feel that letting something go is part of learning to be more tolerant of diversity, or a fear that an employee would become extremely upset if given negative feedback. Unfortunately, letting something go always backfires, as problems worsen and patience wears thin. Employees deserve an accurate appraisal of their performance in relation to the objective standards of the job. Once problems are recognized, they can be dealt with.

Sometimes employees who are from different backgrounds or who have disabilities have a difficult time with an indirect style of supervision. For example, one supervisor of an employee with autism approached the employee and asked, "Would you like to do this for me?" and was shocked when the individual said "No I wouldn't," because the question was meant as a direct order. An employment service agency can consult on supervisory and other support requirements.

It is good practice to give employees, as part of their initial orientation package, a copy of the form with which they will be evaluated. This lets employees know exactly by what standards they will be assessed. Nothing hurts an organization more than performance appraisals that are subjective or arbitrary. Kennedy (1980) recommends having employees evaluate themselves first, then discuss their performance with the supervisor.

Similarly, organizations should have specific written policies covering what is and is not expected of employees and disciplinary steps detailing the consequences of infractions, rather than handling each problem on a case-by-case basis. The more clearly policies are spelled out the more efficiently the organization will run.

Many appraisal formats are a variation on a grid structure, in which components of the job or assessment factors form the rows, and levels of performance form the columns. Employment service agencies generally have a great deal of expertise in the assessment of work behavior. Managers who do not have access to an effective evaluation system may obtain assistance from an agency that is doing business with the company.

When improvement is called for in a worker's performance, setting specific agreed-upon goals is a good idea. When several issues need to be addressed, it is often necessary to isolate and work on the one or two issues that are most important first. Employment service organizations may be called upon to assist in this area as well.

In establishing a partnership between the company and a community rehabilitation program or other employment service agency, it is important that the company maintain clear control over the employment process, utilizing the employment service as a company would engage any other consultant who has specialized expertise in some area. The employment service should be helping build the company's competence in successfully employing a diverse workforce. If, instead, the company finds itself hosting a separate special program, with its own separate performance appraisal system for its clients, neither party is taking full advantage of the expertise of the other partner and it is time to renegotiate the relationship.

ELEMENT 23: PAY DISTRIBUTION
Is there a typical routine for distributing pay within the work area or department?

If there is a routine for distributing pay, then receiving pay in the typical way will be part of what it means to be a full-fledged employee. Pay distribution may also be an occasion for social interactions at work (element #19). Pay day also may be an occasion for employee socializing outside of work (element # 26).

Assessment

Pay is always distributed on a predetermined schedule, whether weekly, biweekly, semimonthly, or monthly. Some companies distribute paychecks or electronic transaction pay stubs by mail. Others hand them out in person, by the supervisor or other designated employee. Simple questioning can determine the procedure used. Observation may be needed to analyze typical interactions that may accompany the distribution of pay.

The possibility of a different manner of pay distribution for a worker will arise only if the worker has some sort of atypical employment status. For example, the worker may be an intern or an apprentice. Or the person may be working under a contract relationship in which the actual employer is a temporary employment agency or a rehabilitation program that pays the worker and bills the company for the individual's services.

Implications for employment assistance

Greater inclusion in the workplace culture will be achieved if employment can be arranged for a worker on the same basis as everyone else. So it is important, first, to find out the purpose a different arrangement is meant to serve, and then investigate whether that purpose can be achieved in some other way. For example, if the primary purpose is to reduce the cost of the employee to the employer, this same outcome can probably be achieved through a mechanism such as an on-the-job training arrangement in which the company is reimbursed for its training time.

Sometimes the purpose of an atypical employment arrangement such as an internship, apprenticeship, or "temp-to-perm" contract is to assist an individual to gain work experience or training that will lead to later employment on a more normative basis. If so, the duration of the work experience should be in writing with clear criteria for the transition.

People who are new to the work force may require assistance in understanding their pay stubs and the workings of employment benefits such as accrual of vacation time, retirement plans, and medical insurance. Employment specialists also should be able to answer basic questions about tax withholdings and filings and to refer consumers to sources of tax assistance.

Implications for management and management consulting

Some employees work at a company in an arrangement sometimes called an "enclave," in which the company pays a single monthly bill to a rehabilitation program and the workers are employed and paid by the program. In this case, the rationale and implications of the arrangement should be considered carefully. If the point is to allow the service to collect "overhead" that is used to pay for a supervisor for the enclave workers, consider whether the company would in general consider it a wise business practice to contract out the supervision of its work force. If this would not typically be done, why is it being done in this situation? If the workers are said to require "special" supervision, try to specify exactly what supervision is needed, and whether or not it is something company personnel already do or could learn to do. If the purpose of the enclave contract is to maintain a close connection between the workers and the employment service for ongoing support purposes, investigate whether the service could make ongoing, regular employment consultation available for company employees with disabilities as an alternative to the current relationship.

ELEMENT 24: CELEBRATIONS

Do workers celebrate any special occasions, such as birthdays?

Many workplaces have customs related to noting a significant event, such as a birthday, wedding, promotion, new baby, etc. Celebrations help build feelings of group solidarity and affiliation. Participation in these celebrations is an important part of belonging to the work group. Even though celebrations may occur only a few times a year, their cultural meaning give celebrations importance that is far out of proportion to their frequency.

Assessment

As with other customs, the details of celebrations and how a person participates in them need to be understood. We may find that some customs are surprisingly complex when we take the time to understand them in detail. For instance, suppose that the day before someone's birthday, his or her nearest co-worker purchases a humorous birthday card and brings it in to work the next day. That individual signs it and adds a witty saying, then gives it to another worker, making sure the individual it is intended for doesn't see it. Each person does the same, until everyone has signed the card. Then it is presented to the individual at lunch time. Does the same person bring the card from person to person, or is each person responsible for determining to whom to give the card next? If a birthday falls on a day off, is it skipped or celebrated on the nearest work day? All of this information is important for a full understanding of the celebration custom. And the card may be only one part of the celebration. And there will be different customs for different types of celebrations.

We celebrate what we value. Therefore the types of events that call for a celebration at a worksite help us understand what is valued there, allowing us to understand other aspects of the culture. For example, if workers celebrate getting a shipment out ahead of schedule, it is a good bet that they value speed and efficiency.

Because celebrations are infrequent, one is unlikely to witness one during a short-term involvement with a worksite. But sometimes clues are visible. A posted worker birthday list is evidence that those dates are celebrated in some way. An "It's a girl! (or boy!)" congratulations sign may remain on the bulletin board for a few weeks. In the absence of this type of clue, a prolonged period of engagement or some questioning of several workers will be needed to assess celebration customs.

Implications for employment assistance

The complexity of some celebration customs – for example, keeping the birthday card hidden from the focal person until the end – can be a fairly complex undertaking. We cannot assume that all workers have the required skills or familiarity with celebration customs in general. One woman with an intellectual disability received a delivery of flowers from her co-workers on her birthday. She went up and hugged the delivery man, thinking that the flowers were from him.

Once celebration customs are understood, an employment specialist can teach the procedures to the employee directly, or can ask a co-worker to show the individual what to do. In the case of behaviors and skills that are performed frequently, such as central work tasks or lunchtime customs, natural opportunities to teach and practice the skills occur regularly. But with infrequently used skills, such as those involved in celebrations (peripheral work tasks and emergency procedures also fall in this category) some individuals will not obtain enough trials to master the skills. Probably the best option is to enlist a co-worker in serving as the worker's guide through the celebration rituals.

If possible, encourage an employee to be an active participant in a celebration, to the degree this is called for by the turn-taking customs at the setting. A worker might, for example, buy the card or cake, make the lunch reservation, or order the flowers. Sometimes these actions, interpreted as thoughtfulness, help cement working relationships.

Implications for management and management consulting

Managers can enable celebrations in small ways, such as maintaining an employee birthday list, allowing workers a little longer for break or to return a little late after a group lunch, and joining in celebrations. Some managers make it a point to find meaningful events that express the values of the work group, such as completing an important contract or meeting a significant production milestone, and organize an appropriate celebration.

ELEMENT 25: COMPANY-SPONSORED SOCIAL ACTIVITIES

Does the company sponsor any social activities, such as an annual picnic, or any sports teams?

Company-sponsored social activities are opportunities for workers to get to know one another in a context that is enjoyable and less stressful than work. Usually participation is optional rather than mandatory from the perspective of formal job requirements, but may not be optional from the perspective of joining the culture. Social activities may be either during or outside of work time.

Assessment

Some companies host one or two annual social events, such as a picnic or holiday party. Others sponsor ongoing activities, such as bowling, softball, or other sports teams. Midsize and large companies are sometimes associated with a charitable foundation or involved in a social or civic cause that has some associated activity workers participate in, such as a fund-raising "walkathon." Workers who have been with the organization for a while can be a source of information about any of these activities. Sometimes bulletin boards, company newsletters, and annual reports are an additional source of information.

Implications for employment assistance

Employment staff can point out opportunities and the benefits of participation to consumers. It may be necessary to help an employee work out arrangements to have the money and the transportation needed to participate in company-sponsored social activities.

Sometimes a part-time or temporary worker, such as an intern, will be left out of the invitation "loop" out of simple thoughtlessness, for instance, someone forgot that the individual was off duty when the announcement was made. Advocacy is needed to ensure that the worker feels welcome to participate. And for any new employee, a general announcement or notice may need to be followed up with a personal invitation or suggestion from a member of the work group. As with other social customs (e.g., element #20), the particular behaviors necessary for participation need to be understood and explained or shown to the worker.

Implications for management and management consulting

Sponsorship of social activities fosters and enhances group cohesion. Not every worker who wishes to attend may be able to arrange transportation to an activity, so ride-sharing can be encouraged.

One of the difficulties employees with disabilities or those who are members of a minority group historically have experienced is being viewed by others in a one-dimensional or stereotypical way, such that the disability or the minority status is far too large a part of the individual's identity. Participation in activities in which workers become known in different contexts and see different sides of one another can be part of the process of breaking down the barriers to full acceptance.

In the case of employees with disabilities, many are viewed by society as primarily recipients of charitable help. When a company has connections to a charitable or social cause, involving workers with disabilities as active participants in the cause and as givers of help to others sends a powerful message that helps dispel this stereotype.

ELEMENT 26: OUTSIDE ACTIVITIES

Do workers ever get together as a group after work or on their days off?

Such activities as attending "happy hour" at a customary establishment after work are informal work group customs, not the sort of company-sponsored events covered in element #25. A supervisor or department head may take part in the activity, but as an individual, not in his or her formal capacity. Social activities outside of work are evidence of a strong bond among the members of a work group. They provide additional opportunities for employees to get to know one another more personally.

Assessment

Going out after work for a beer on payday, or going to an exercise class once a week at lunch hour are examples of non-company-sponsored, "grassroots" social activities that may become customs. Subgroups or cliques may participate, rather than an entire work group.

Sometimes people underreport the strength of their adherence an outside activity custom. A worker might say something such as, "A few of us go out for a beer now and again, when we feel like it," whereas the observable reality is that they do this every Friday without fail. People may of course be deliberately misleading. But a common and more innocent explanation is that participation in a custom that is freely entered into each time may not be consciously experienced as "following a custom." It is just that every Friday at about the same time the individual happens to feel that going out for a beer with some co-workers sounds like a good idea at that particular moment. Prolonged engagement with a work group, what we have called Phase 3 of information gathering (page 12), may be needed to assess this element.

Keep in mind that worker privacy regarding activities outside of work needs to be respected. It may be a good idea to phrase questions in terms of the group, e.g., "Does the group ever go out after work?". Reiterate that your purpose is to help someone fit in with the group, so you are interested only in information that relates to that goal. Otherwise, when you ask about outside activities, workers may feel that you are prying into their personal lives.

What makes something a custom, as opposed to an isolated instance of people doing something, is the regularity and predictability of its occurrence, along with some social meaning that is associated with the activity. The predictable or routine nature of a custom should be observable – every Friday, whenever the truck pulls up, at lunch, and so on. But equally important is that those in the setting view the activity as routine – that *they* predict it. For example, if one worker says to another, "Where were you last Friday? I didn't see you at Charlie's," that is a piece of evidence supporting the hypothesis that going to Charlie's on Friday is customary. Social meaning is difficult to define, but people tend to know it when they see it. For example, if one gets the sense that members of the group use going to Charlie's on Friday as a way of "winding down" from the work week, or use it to "drown their sorrows" or to fulfill some other shared function, then it has social meaning.

Implications for employment assistance

Usually people begin participating in activities outside of work as a result of a specific invitation, so there may be opportunities to ask someone if they would consider inviting a new person. A co-worker who is serving as an employee's mentor (element # 11) would be ideal for this function.

An employment specialist has to use a certain amount of judgment and intuition regarding whether to seek out a co-worker and ask, as opposed to holding off and seeing if someone issues a spontaneous invitation. There is no "instruction sheet" to turn to for guidance. Employment specialists need to be able to trust that they possess the relevant intuition to an acceptable degree. As a successful employee yourself, your intuitive "feel" for a situation, based on your experience and your sizing up of the people involved, is likely to be correct.

As with element #25, having enough money and having reliable transportation may be issues influencing whether or not an employee can participate in social activities outside of work. With experience, workers become accustomed to the necessity of investing back, so to speak, some of their earned income in clothing, transportation, haircuts, lunch money, and other "costs of doing business" as an employee. Less experienced employees may need specific assistance and advice in this area.

Implications for management and management consulting

The development and maintenance of a group custom for social activity outside of work depends primarily on individual personalities and interests. As a rule, these activities should be regarded as a welcome sign of group cohesion. Other than decide as individuals whether to participate or not, there is little that managers can or should do to either facilitate or discourage them.

ELEMENT 27: EMPLOYEE ASSISTANCE AND WELLNESS PROGRAMS

Does the company sponsor or assist with an Employee Assistance Program or wellness program?

Employee Assistance Programs (EAPs) assist employees who, due to life problems, are having difficulty with their job performance. About 5,000 EAPs exist in the US (Hanley-Maxwell, Bordieri, and Merz, 1996). Some large companies have their own in-house EAP but most companies contract for EAP services from a separate organization serving more than one business.

Wellness programs can range from conducting stretching exercise routines at a workplace or hosting a lecture about quitting smoking to an extensive array of offerings, such as information and classes on diet and health, a company gym, or prevention programs tied to an employer's health maintenance/medical insurance plan. The availability of an EAP or wellness program evidences a commitment to investing in human resources on the part of an employer.

Assessment

The personnel or human resources department will have information about a company's EAP or wellness program. Various other names are sometimes applied to a wellness program, such as an "exercise program" or "prevention program," so it is best to ask for and obtain descriptive information. Employers that are too small to have a personnel or human resources department are unlikely to offer such programs, but it is wise to check with the management to be sure. It is important to investigate how and to what extent a program is used, and how employees access the program, to make sure it doesn't exist only "on paper." It is easier to obtain information of this kind from workers about a wellness program than an EAP, because most EAP utilization is private and confidential.

Implications for employment assistance

An employer's own wellness and EAP programs are sources of job support for employees, and thus any employee who requires significant job supports should take full advantage of them within the scope of the program's expertise. Many reasonable accommodations required by employees with disabilities can be provided by existing programs.

Traditionally, EAPs have been associated with alcoholism and drug abuse assistance and with mental health problems. Thus EAP personnel may be most suited to assistance with this type of issue. But there is no reason why, in collaboration with a community rehabilitation program, an EAP could not expand the scope of its services and provide a wider array of job accommodation services, information and referral services, and other related assistance to employees with disabilities. Some creative community rehabilitation services even offer Employee Assistance Programming as one of their services to employers. When assisting someone to utilize an EAP service, it is important to respect the confidentiality of information provided to the EAP counselor, since the assurance of confidentiality is one of the cornerstones of the success of this type of program.

Wellness programs can serve a number of purposes for an employee, depending on their specific offerings and services. One worker concerned about being overweight and not having enough stamina to work full-time attended a series of company-sponsored weight loss and exercise workshops and after several months was able to increase his hours to full-time.

Implications for management and management consulting

Employee assistance and wellness programs have expanded rapidly in popularity, and for a simple reason. The costs to a company of poor employee performance, absenteeism, and job turnover can be enormous, and these programs have a good track record of success in reducing them (Hanley-Maxwell, Bordieri, and Merz, 1996).

Employment service staff have, in addition to their consultation and support services to business, one foot in the human service world. As such they have a wealth of useful contacts and information. For instance, they may be in a position to do some of the initial legwork involved in identifying EAP providers with the highest quality services. Employment service staff also may be of assistance as consultants to an in-house EAP, for example, as a source of information and referral for community rehabilitation services.

Smaller or medium businesses often can benefit from pooling resources and information. For example, several businesses can form an employer consortium (Balser, Harvey, and Hornby, 1998) to share ideas, strategies, and information related to supporting individuals with mental illness in the workplace. Often when one business finds itself faced with a problem, another business has already figured out the solution.

ELEMENT 28: CAR POOLING/TRANSPORTATION

Does the company assist employees with car pooling or provide public transit discounts or similar transportation assistance?

Employee benefits of this kind are a sign of a strong company commitment to its work force. The specific type of assistance varies widely across businesses and communities. Transportation assistance is also evidence that the business is aware that a diverse workforce is likely to include some individuals who do not have access to a private automobile for transportation to work.

Assessment

The first order of business in assessing this element is to take a look in general at how people travel back and forth from their homes to the work setting, by asking a few workers about their transportation. One also can notice whether a bus or other transit stop is located near the workplace. Management can provide information about any employer assistance or subsidies the company provides for transportation. Free parking should not, for the purposes of this analysis, be considered a type of transportation assistance. If there is a serious carpooling effort in place, one may find evidence of it in the form of notices or information on a bulletin board or in the company newsletter.

Implications for employment assistance

The availability of transportation to work should be taken into account long before an employee has a job offer, during career planning and in the job search. Some workers will be able to seriously consider only companies that either provide transportation assistance, are in their immediate neighborhood, or are otherwise accessible.

A worker may have the option of beginning a job with an employment specialist initially providing transportation and then search for a co-worker willing to assume this function. This strategy is extremely risky. If it fails, it puts the employment assistance agency in the position of choosing to either permanently become a transportation service or to appear inconsiderate and unprofessional to both the employer and the employee.

It is usually possible for an employment specialist to help a worker make use of whatever transportation assistance a company has available, even if this involves some modification or adaptation of the usual system. For example, an employee who does not drive might join a car pool and arrange to pay for some of the gas instead of taking a turn with the driving.

There are many ways for individuals with disabilities to learn to drive, to take and pass driving tests, and to physically drive a car, so this option should not be dismissed without thorough examination. Individuals with expertise in driver education assessment are often available through an assistive technology office, vocational rehabilitation office, or community college. And driving a car need not be an "all or nothing" proposition. For example, some individuals are able to safely and confidently learn a "back way" to and from work, where less traffic is encountered.

Not being able to drive does not automatically mean that it makes no sense to own a car. Some individuals are able to purchase or lease a vehicle using various combinations of earned income; savings; Social Security Plans for Achieving Self Support; inheritance, settlement, or other lump-sum payments; and state vocational rehabilitation or welfare-to-work office funding. With a vehicle, these individuals are able to negotiate creative transportation arrangements, such as for one or more co-workers to drive the individual and their vehicle back and forth to work, thereby saving on their own transportation expenses.

It is advisable to refer an individual who incurs transportation expenses because of a disability to someone knowledgeable about the income tax and Social Security implications of these expenses. A variety of deductions and "disregards" are available.

Implications for management and management consulting

It has become so commonplace for most adults to drive and have access to a car that many aspects of our culture in general have been built around this easy access to personal automobile travel. But there remain many adults who for one reason or another don't drive or have access to a car. Yet these individuals possess important skills and talents that businesses need. When a company is inaccessible by public transportation, planning for workforce diversity should include a recognition of the need for a positive approach to transportation assistance. A bulletin board for ride-sharing is a low cost strategy. Some companies even have found that it pays them to provide worker transportation. It is important to keep in mind that even if the company is accessible by public transportation, some planning may be required to match shift times to bus schedules and to make sure the bus system is usable by people with disabilities.

In planning for transportation, as with many other areas of diversity management and employee support, businesses benefit by networking with other businesses. For instance, two nearby businesses jointly may be able to offer vastly more carpooling options than either business alone. And businesses can wield more clout together or through their business associations than separately. For example, the collective voice of the business community may be able to tip the scales in favor of community spending to extend, improve, or inaugurate public transportation, and thus make those businesses accessible to a wider range of potential employees.

ELEMENT 29: EMPLOYEE INCENTIVES
Does the employer utilize any employee incentives or awards programs?

When this element is present, participation in these programs is likely to form a part of the workplace culture. Incentive or awards programs may express a concern for employee job satisfaction, or a desire to work in partnership with employees in meeting productivity or sales goals.

Assessment

Employee recognition can be given for "Employee of the Month," "Best Suggestion for Improving Productivity," or any number of other possibilities. These can be accompanied by a monetary award, or a "perk" such as a preferred parking space or gift certificate. Productivity incentives can include bonuses, such as a salary supplement for exceeding productivity goals or an end-of-the-year or holiday bonus, or a profit-sharing plan. Some retail establishments offer employee discounts. All of these should also be considered as employee incentives.

A conversation with company management will be necessary to understand the basic outlines of any company incentive or awards program. It is also a good idea to ask employees about the program as well, since they may have a different perspective than management. There also may be customs associated with the giving and receiving of awards that are important to understand. Only positive incentives should be included in this assessment, not disincentives such as docking or dismissal. Neither should regular wages, benefits, good working conditions, and opportunities for training be considered in assessing this element.

Implications for employment assistance

Staff providing employment assistance should advocate for inclusion of an employee in whatever incentives or awards programs are available at a workplace. If an individual requires assistance in becoming proficient or learning to increase work speed, existing employer incentive programs can sometimes be helpful natural reinforcers. For example, an employee can establish a series of productivity objectives (such as two boxes a day, then three boxes a day, and so on) that are tied to achieving "Employee of the Month" status or some other incentive.

Implications for management and management consulting

Employee incentives usually turn out to be a surprisingly inexpensive way to boost morale and productivity. It is important that desired levels of productivity be objectively defined and be achievable without distress or injury. A goal that is achievable by all workers supports a healthy workplace culture more than a system in which individuals compete against one another to see who "wins." Such a system can result in conflict relationships or even sabotage. By contrast, in pursuing an objective criteria, employees "compete" against their own current level of performance rather than against one another. Another approach is to set group rather than individual goals or deadlines and provide awards or recognition to a work group.

A policy of giving a bonus simply because it is a tradition, independent of anyone's work behavior, may be useful as a form of celebration but it risks turning into a "dissatisfier" rather than a "satisfier." A removal of a dissatisfier never can turn into a satisfier. In other words, workers will come to view not getting a bonus or getting less of a bonus one year than the previous year as a source of complaint and dissatisfaction, while getting the bonus will simply be expected.

It is useful to distinguish between providing incentives for outcomes (such as increased sales or product quality) and incentives for effort (such as more time devoted to customer contact or more thorough inspection). In general, a focus on outcomes places the management emphasis in the right place, as long as the selected outcomes are things largely under the employees' control.

ELEMENT 30: WORK/FAMILY POLICIES

Do company policies include any supportive work/family programs such as flextime or dependent care assistance?

In the past decade work/family issues have become increasingly important in the workplace. We are moving towards a society in which all of the adults in most families are employed, and each employee must find some way to balance family and work life. Those companies with explicit work/family policies see the connection between maintaining a "user-friendly" workplace culture and accomplishing business objectives. By respecting the different needs of different employees and their families, good work/family policies have a way of blending the needs of the individual with the needs of the group. The employee fits in with the culture, but the culture also fits in with the employee.

Assessment

Both the number of companies with work/family policies and the types of work/family arrangements being offered are growing steadily. Examples of work/family policies are child care subsidies or on-site child care, provision for flexible scheduling or working at home via "telecommuting," provision for leave time or "sabbaticals" to address family or personal needs, and pretax spending accounts for dependent care. Some innovative companies even provide personal services like shopping for their employees. Human resource or personnel offices are able to provide information about written policies. The first-line managers in a workplace should be consulted as well, because some individual managers may informally allow a degree of flexibility and responsiveness to individual circumstances beyond what is reflected in the written policies.

Implications for employment assistance

Work/family policies usually are developed for the benefit of current employees of a company. But many of the flexible policies being introduced can play a role in eliminating barriers to employment for individuals who have traditionally been underrepresented in the workforce as well. Thus, work/family policies can play a role in job development and job negotiations for an employee who may have individual accommodation requirements. For example, one individual whose medications made it difficult for him to stay awake before late morning was able to arrange a flextime schedule that took advantage of his individual situation.

All employees at least potentially can benefit from company work/family policies, so it is important to ensure that an employee is able to take advantage of them when needed to the same degree as other employees. This might mean taking care to explain and periodically remind an individual of what is available, or assisting the individual to make a request to company management. Assistance can range from talking over or rehearsing the discussion to accompanying the individual or making the request on his or her behalf. Even though employees may have been informed about a policy, at the time when an employee is experiencing a problem or a change in family circumstances he or she might need to be reminded of the availability of assistance and how to request it.

Implications for management and management consulting

Some companies try out an innovative arrangement, such as child care "scholarships" to a community preschool program, on an experimental basis. They evaluate its benefits against the costs before making a final decision. Other arrangements, such as flexible scheduling, may not have direct financial implications but may have other, possibly hidden, costs.

Flextime and telecommuting, for instance, will affect a workplace culture in that they will reduce opportunities for shared schedules (element #5) and all of the activities that flow from shared presence at the worksite. For this reason, some companies have required that all employees spend one or two days per week on-site. It is particularly important in such a situation to ensure that on-site time is "quality time" for workers in terms of shared breaks (element #9) or meals (element #8), staff meetings (element #21), celebrations (element #24), and other cultural practices.

Some businesses were initially concerned that compliance with the "reasonable accommodation" requirement for an employee with a disability under the Americans with Disabilities Act might be burdensome and complicated. But those companies with a tradition of work/family flexibility often find that "reasonable accommodation" means nothing more ominous than applying the same flexible approach to job designs and work schedules that is already standard practice with any employee.

ELEMENT 31: OPPORTUNITIES FOR ADVANCEMENT

Is there evidence of advancement or promotion of some workers from entry level to higher positions within the company?

Companies with what labor economists refer to as an "internal labor market" – a career ladder along which an individual can be promoted to jobs with increasing levels of responsibility and higher salaries – offer more possibilities for advancement. Workers are able to learn about other potentially interesting jobs. Managers are able to observe and select potential candidates to fill job openings from within.

Assessment

The best assessment of an internal labor market is to ask several managers or senior-level employees how they started with the company. If at least one of the people you ask has advanced from within the company, this will provide the strongest evidence that people do in fact work their way up the ladder. The existence of a serious commitment to employee training (element #11) also will support the hypothesis that opportunity for advancement is an element of a workplace culture. When advancement does occur, attention should be given to any promotion rituals or ceremonies.

Implications for employment assistance

If an individual is seriously interested in moving up within a company and is considering taking an entry-level job primarily to gain entry to other jobs, there should be a specific discussion with the employer prior to accepting the job. This should include what other jobs this initial job prepares one for, what should be expected in terms of the length of time one is likely to remain at entry-level, and the proficiency to be achieved before promotion is considered. You then can have a similar discussion as part of the periodic employee performance review (element #22).

Many times an individual will begin a job with a few core duties. As these are learned, more will be added. This process is sometimes called horizontal, rather than vertical, promotion. Employment assistance can include making suggestions to the employer and employee about new tasks to try out, and employment service staff can offer to assist by analyzing the new task, suggesting any adaptations if needed or offering to assist with the training. Once new tasks are added, the employment service staff may have a role to play as an employee's advocate or, in effect, "agent," making sure that the employer is well aware of the new accomplishments, and that the individual is able to request and receive salary increases as warranted.

Another important aspect of career advancement is the transition to increasing amounts of autonomy and responsibility, rather than the simple carrying out of a procedure that is common in an entry-level job. Employment specialists can assist with this process by making sure that an employee is introduced to the context in which his or her work is performed – the "big picture." He or she also should be provided with a graduated series of problem-solving situations that represent opportunities to figure out a solution, ask for help when needed, and be in charge of achieving an outcome.

Implications for management and management consulting

Perhaps the ideal career advancement situation is a hierarchy of positions at a company such that mastery of each level sets the stage for movement to the next level. A careful analysis of the essential functions of each job position may help in establishing this type of hierarchy.

At the same time, advancement ought not be mandatory. One might qualify for one job and do it well without ever qualifying for the next higher job. Advancement also may occur horizontally within a given job by adding additional responsibilities and tasks to enrich the scope of the job. Assigning an exemplary employee as a mentor for new employees is a good example of this type of job enrichment.

Part III
The Workplace
Culture Survey

The Workplace Culture Survey is a tool designed to analyze and assess how the thirty-one elements of workplace culture work together at a given work setting, and the degree to which an individual is included in a workplace culture. In the Appendix are all the questions that appear in the survey. A copy of the full survey in booklet form was included with this book. You can purchase additional copies of the survey from the publisher.

The survey consists of two parts. Part A is Strength of Workplace Culture . Part B is Level of Workplace Inclusion.

The questions in Part A ask about each element of workplace culture. For simplicity, a "yes" or "no" answer should be provided for each element, indicating whether or not that specific element is present or absent at the work setting being analyzed. If the answer to a question does not seem to be unequivocally either "yes" or "no," think of a "no" answer as encompassing "to a negligible degree or importance" and "yes" as equivalent to "to a noteworthy degree or importance."

A "yes" answer directs attention to an element as relevant to inclusion in that work setting. The total number of "yes" answers, a number between zero and thirty-one, provides a rough measure of what we might call the strength of a workplace culture. A higher number indicates a stronger culture, with more possibilities for inclusion, support, and relationships.

To the right of the "yes/no" answer column in the survey booklet, a column is provided for entering a description or explanation of the details of the culture. This information will be far more important for planning and decision-making than the simple "yes/no." For example, it is useful to know that some special terms and language are used at a worksite (element #13), but it is far more useful to know what those terms are.

An element that cannot be answered one way or another should be left blank. It is usually necessary to complete the Workplace Culture Survey in phases, so elements left blank may be filled in later as more information is collected.

Part B can help in planning for and assessing the inclusion of a specific individual into the culture of a workplace. For each element in Part A, a corresponding question in Part B asks whether the individual participates in or is included in that element. Again, a "yes" or "no" answer is called for. So in tricky or borderline situations, such as when a person "sort of" participates in a custom, it is important to determine which answer fits best, or which way you tend to lean towards more.

A "yes" answer should be given only if the focal individual's participation matches the description that has been given of that element in Part A to a reasonable degree. For example, if the company provides an orientation session for new employees, a general outline of the orientation should be entered in the appropriate column next to element #10. Then, answer "yes" to the corresponding inclusion question only if the individual you are considering participated in that same orientation. If the individual did have an orientation, but it was a substantially different kind of orientation, the answer is "no."

The last column allows an opportunity to plan strategies for job modification or employment consultation, in any situation where a "yes" on the left or Part A side is accompanied by a "no" on the right or Part B side. The implications of each element for employment specialist practice and for company management or management consulting provided in Part II of this book may be helpful in developing a strategy.

An overall level of inclusion score is obtained by counting the number of items with a "yes" answer to both the left-hand and right-hand (a and b) versions of each question. More "yes" matches indicate greater inclusion into the culture. So the total count of "yes" matches – ranging from zero to thirty-one – is a rough measure of the inclusion of an individual.

One also can calculate the percentage or proportion of "yes" responses in Part A that also are answered "yes" in Part B. The purpose of the assessment should dictate which procedure to follow. If a work setting scores twenty in the strength of its culture, an employee with twenty "yes" answers in Part B is maximally included, whereas an employee in a work setting with a thirty rating for the strength of its culture who scores a twenty-five in inclusion has a way to go before being fully included. So one way of summarizing the situation would be to say that the first employee is 100% included while the second is only 75% included. But from the perspective of career development and overall quality of life, we can view the second employee as included in twenty-five different elements of a strong workplace culture that has additional elements to become included in, while the first employee has reached a cultural dead-end at twenty.

Reliability and Validity

Two people analyzing the same workplace using the Workplace Culture Survey will see and hear different things, interpret what they see and hear differently, and quite possibly arrive at somewhat different scores. There is an inevitable degree of subjectivity involved in analyzing a workplace culture. The scores that can be obtained through the instrument for strength of workplace culture and level of workplace inclusion therefore must be considered as only very rough approximations. The Workplace Culture Survey is primarily useful as a planning tool – a checklist of elements of workplace culture and space for recording details and plans. This can be achieved even if the computation of scores is ignored. But sometimes even a very rough comparison of cultures at different worksites, of the same worksite at different points in time, or of the level of inclusion before and after some intervention is better than nothing. The development and field-testing of the survey included consideration of the reliability and validity of workplace culture scores.

Construct Validity

The Workplace Culture Survey was developed from a comprehensive review of business and sociology literature related to organizational and workplace culture, each element matching one cultural feature of a work setting noted in the literature. In addition, several existing instruments were examined that assess organizational culture or workplace social inclusion, and nonduplicate elements of workplace culture in those instruments were added. The following instruments were used:

- *The Culture Audit* (Thomas, 1991)
- *Job Analysis* (McLaughlin, Garner, and Callahan, 1986)
- *Vocational Integration Inventory* (Parent, Kregel, Wehman, and Metzler, 1991)
- *Work Environment Scale* (Moos and Insel, 1974)
- *The Work-Family Corporate Environment Scan* (Pitt-Catsouphes and Mirvis, 1994)

The draft instrument was then compared with fieldnote data from a qualitative study of supported employment settings (Hagner, 1989) to ensure that aspects of the culture found to be important for the inclusion of workers with disabilities in that study were captured adequately. The Workplace Culture Survey was then field-tested in a statewide demonstration project (Hagner and Faris, 1994). Some of the wording of items was revised and the survey was simplified, based on user input.

Concurrent Validity

Workplace Inclusion scores were compared with data from an in-depth qualitative study of a sample of six work settings employing an individual with a severe disability (Butterworth, Hagner, Helm, and Whelley, 1999). The inclusion of supported employees at the six work settings was rank ordered from most inclusive to least inclusive based on an analysis of co-worker interactions and supports described in the narrative field notes. The same settings were rank ordered based on workplace inclusion scores on the independently completed Workplace Culture Surveys. The two rankings were identical.

Inter-rater Reliability

The Workplace Culture Survey was administered independently by two different observers during simultaneous visits to the same six work settings. Even though the two observers were often in different parts of the setting or interacted with different people, the ratings given by the two observers for the strength of workplace culture and workplace Inclusion agreed in 293 out of 395 possible elements, or 74.2% agreement.

Conducting the Survey

To complete the survey, data are collected to answer thirty-one questions by means of on-site observations and conversations with workers and managers. Some questions are harder to answer than others. Some questions apply more to some worksites than they do to others. Every workplace has to be approached on its own terms.

Three visits of about an hour and a half each is a good rule of thumb for completing most of the survey at most workplaces, but this is only a rough estimate. Some questions may be answerable without visiting, such as by talking with a former employee. And others may require prolonged exposure to find the answer.

If there is no self-evident "work group" or "work area," use your best judgment to bound the scope of the assessment. At many settings it makes sense to consider all the workers supervised by one supervisor as one work group. But one will run across exceptions to this rule

– two distinct groups who share the same supervisor, or a group of workers who do not share the same supervisor yet function as one group. To answer questions about what "workers" or "most workers" do, you can obtain the answer by asking either three or five workers (an odd number so there can't be a tie) and using the majority answer.

The objective in conducting visits to assess a workplace culture is to blend in so that people are going about their everyday routines and not reacting to the presence of an observer. There is no way to ever be sure that one has achieved this. In fact it probably never is completely achieved – remember that Flyonda Wall is no longer with us – only approximated to varying degrees. Using some of the following strategies improves the approximation.

1. Find a spot to hang out in and appear uninteresting. The ideal spot is one that isn't in anyone's way, yet affords a good view of the work setting or allows you to hear some of what is going on. If no one spot is ideal, use a sampling strategy: Remain in one spot for a while, then move to another that has a different vantage point. Some time will be required before the setting acclimates to your presence. As you may have noticed if you have tried to photograph people, they tend to act "on stage" when they first realize someone is looking at them. But if you hold the camera long enough, you outlast people's stamina for keeping this on-stage persona up. You fade into the background of their perception, and they begin to act as if there was no observer.

2. Explain your presence to people in a relaxed way that assures them that your observations cannot affect them, that you are of no importance to them. If people are not sure of this (if they suspect, for instance, that you might "tell" on them if they were to stand around not working) they probably will not act natural. Instead they will do whatever they think they need to do to stay out of trouble. If you then observe them working hard, you don't know how to interpret it. An example of a relatively innocuous reason for being there is "to learn more about this kind of work" or "to see what it would be like working here." If you are there in connection with a specific employee, "I'm here to help with Sarah's training" or "Joe asked me to look at his job and see if I had any ideas about how he could fit in better" should suffice. Keep in mind that you may have to explain your presence over and over to each person you meet.

If at all possible, adopt a policy of never reporting specific observations. Use findings for no other purpose than to suggest or plan inclusion strategies or to suggest or plan management initiatives that enhance the culture. If you must violate this policy – for example, if you observe harassment and the only way to put a stop to it is report it – you also must retire as a neutral collector of cultural data at that workplace.

3. As you begin to learn the culture, you become better able to figure out what else you need to see. For example, once you become oriented to social times (element #6) and gathering places (element #7), you can plan to hang out in that place at those times to assess social interactions (element #19) and other elements.

4. Conducting an analysis of relevant jobs and filling out job analysis forms, again while looking as uninteresting as possible, often creates an easily understandable role and rationale for being at a worksite. Workplace culture analysis (of the social aspects of the job) and job analysis (of the work tasks and requirements) go hand in hand. So, they can be completed together for the purpose of "finding out about the various jobs here." A good job analysis format can be found in McLaughlin, Garner, and Callahan (1986).

5. Sometimes you can identify a way to be marginally useful at a setting, without really becoming viewed as a worker. For instance, you can straighten something or make something neater. Make sure, first, that what you do actually is helping and not creating more work for someone, and also that you do not become so useful that people start counting on you or giving you more work to do.

6. At visits to some work settings you can fit in as a customer. For example, you can watch a receptionist from a waiting room, or listen to workplace interactions at a hairdressing salon while having your hair done.

7. Some employment service organizations define and market themselves to employers in a way that makes it natural to visit a work setting as a consultant or in some similar role. For example, one might visit a company for a day as a way of get-

ting some background information in preparation for an employee training session on workplace diversity. It may be difficult in this type of situation to project a sense of being unimportant and unable to affect anything, because you are beginning to intervene as soon as you take on a consultant role.

In a situation where you suspect that there might be some reactivity of the setting to your presence, and you have no better option, it may be possible to "factor in" how people might be acting differently. For example, if you suspect that people are wondering whether you might be observing their work output to see if they are being efficient, you can assume that they are being overly conscientious about their efficiency and disregard the observation that they are working efficiently. But during lunch break, when efficiency is not an issue, there should be no reason for these workers to change from their usual topics of conversation, so those lunchtime behaviors can be assumed to be unaffected.

The Workplace Culture Survey usually is completed a little at a time, over several visits. The process can be divided into roughly three phases: job application and interview, initial training and adjustment, and ongoing support. This means that the survey can be conveniently conducted in many cases without additional time demands. An employment specialist probably already will be planning to visit a worksite for these purposes. Attending to the culture might be a new way of structuring what to look for and add a new level of awareness to workplace visits, but it does not necessarily involve a new set of visits.

Frequently a Workplace Culture Survey will be underway but only Phase 1 of data collection is complete by the time an applicant must decide whether or not to accept a job offer. It is not feasible for an observer to spend enough time in advance at the setting to learn about all thirty-one elements in detail. The decision must be based on only partial information about the culture, running the obvious risk that information discovered later will show that the setting was a poor fit.

There are several strategies that one can consider in situations where it is important to collect as much cultural information as possible up-front:

- An organization can help form and work with an Employer Consortium (Balser, Harvey and Hornby, 1998) or a similar group of employers who are committed to becoming better able to accommodate workers with disabilities. From participation in a consortium, companies gain not only access to a pool of workers, but an increased ability to manage a diverse workforce. As part of their pursuit of this goal, companies can work to analyze their workplace cultures, with consultation and guidance. Consortium businesses then become in an important sense clients of the employment service organization. Employment service staff are already familiar with various departments, facilities, and their workplace cultures at the time a job decision needs to be made.

- An employment service agency can use personal networking contacts, people who are both receptive to the goals of the organization and who have personal connections to company management, as intermediaries to help "break in" to the company (Nietupski, Murray, Chappelle, Strang, Steele, and Egli, 1993). For instance, an advocate might be able to arrange a meeting with top management. This meeting may lead to a series of visits to look at one or more departments and analyze jobs. Through this process, the employment service will obtain multiple opportunities to observe work settings and departments in connection with developing proposals or examining opportunities. Eventually, it will achieve a solid understanding of workplace cultures at the business.

- On a smaller scale, personal connections can be used to drive a job search. The connections can be those of staff members or the consumer. Often canvassing social networks turns up someone who can provide "inside" information about a company of interest. For instance, it may be that your neighbor or a member of the job seeker's religious congregation once worked for a certain company and knows what working there is like.

- Some employment service organizations broker job sharing arrangements whereby an employee without a disability, sometimes called a "paid co-worker" (Hood, Test, Spooner, and Steele, 1996), is selected jointly by the employment service and the employer. This individual has a dual role, as a worker with production skills and responsibilities and also as a supportive co-worker assisting an employee with a disability, who also is hired by the company. This individual can complete the Workplace Culture Survey as a start-up function in connection with becoming acclimated to the company. This information can be used to help plan supports for the other worker.

Frequently Asked Questions about Workplace Cultures

Looking at work settings from the perspective of workplace culture can give richness and depth to the understanding of a workplace, but until one gains some experience with it, questions may arise during the process of culture analysis and inclusion planning. Below are responses to the most frequently asked questions.

What if some information about a culture is contradictory? Sometimes two or more pieces of information about a workplace culture conflict with one another, leading to confusion about what the "real" culture is. For example, the supervisor may say, "We emphasize teamwork here," and talk about worker collaboration. But workers seem to be competing against one another and never are observed working as a team.

In general, what people do has to be given more weight than what they say. But if words and deeds are in conflict, it may be important to analyze the mismatch further. The culture may contain a rule that can be stated something like this: "Talk about teamwork in certain contexts to cover up the fact that this is a 'dog-eat-dog' operation." This a complex rule to follow – and it is likely that this in itself a problem for some workers. But more importantly, it can be an emotionally stressful rule to follow, and this fact will have a deep impact on a workplace culture. If conflicts are noted, and especially if most other "worker-friendly" elements of the culture such as elements #25 to #30 are missing or if longevity is low (element #1), one may be dealing with a "toxic workplace" (Pfeffer, 1998) with a very weak culture. If one conflict is noted in an otherwise strong, healthy culture, the best course of action is probably to leave the one item blank for the time being and collect more information.

Another good rule of thumb when faced with a puzzle is to directly pose your puzzle to the people in the setting and ask for their help in clearing it up. Unless one has inadvertently stepped on a sensitive area, workers may be happy to be asked and glad to volunteer information. Keep in mind that as an outside observer you will see only a small fraction of what goes on over a small span of time. It is not surprising that it will not all fit together neatly. Most of the context and meaning of what you observe has to be drawn from your respondents – the people in the setting you talk to who seem trustworthy.

Is it important for an employee to be included in everything? In completing the Workplace Culture Survey, there may be several "no" answers to elements of the culture on the Part B side of the survey that were answered "yes" in Part A. This in itself does not necessarily indicate a problem. Workplace inclusion is not an all or nothing issue, but a matter of degree. It would be difficult for any one individual to fit in perfectly with each and every element of a workplace culture. In fact, some level of individuality may be valued by a workplace culture. Pure conformity, paradoxically, would not fit in. The only guide available to help determine which elements are more important to be included in, or what the threshold is for how many things one needs to be included in, is the workplace culture itself.

Wanous (1992) makes a useful distinction between *pivotal* and *relevant* organizational values. Pivotal values must be adhered to, whereas relevant values are optional. An employee who disregards one or two relevant values might be thought of as a "creative individualist," whereas someone who disregards a pivotal value is at risk of being regarded as not fitting in. This same distinction probably applies to all elements of workplace culture.

Therefore, while each "no" on Part B next to a "yes" on Part A of the survey lowers the resulting level of inclusion rating by one, a high but less-than-perfect rating is not always a bad thing. A low score, on the other hand, does indicate a problem. An effort should be made to identify a few elements of the culture where inclusion can be facilitated. But this should not be done merely to raise a score. For each element, one should consider carefully its importance within the overall culture, the consequences (both good and bad) of not fitting in with that specific element, and the feasibility and potential side-effects of whatever interventions might be used to facilitate inclusion in that element.

If nothing can be done about a lack of inclusion in one or more fairly important elements of a workplace culture, sometimes concentrating heavily on facilitating inclusion in those elements that can be impacted can overcome that one discrepancy. For example, in a certain law office the first hour or so of work is a more social time (element # 6) and the afternoon is very busy. An individual with a severe disability is being offered a job as a photocopier during the busy afternoon hours only. A "yes" on Question A6 and a "no" on B6 seems unavoidable. One can begin the job in this way with a long-term employment consulting goal of finding some meaningful morning task to add to the job later. Meanwhile, one can pay especially close attention to inclusion in other areas that relate to interacting socially with co-workers, such as gathering places (element #7) and lunch (element #8).

Can someone be "over-included"? Sometimes one employee is in a position of doing or having more of something than most co-workers – for instance, having a personalized work space (element #18) when most other workers do not, having a more thorough orientation (element #10) than others, or having greater longevity (element #1) than most other workers. Are these situations examples of "extra inclusion" or of non-inclusion?

The workplace inclusion (Part B) questions are deliberately worded to refer back to the corresponding questions in Part A. For example, Question B10 asks whether an employee participated in the same orientation as other workers. If an orientation was provided for only the individual, the correct answer for question B10 is "no." There is no possibility of "extra credit."

This does not mean that the orientation was a bad idea, only that it did not contribute to inclusion in the culture. We have seen that one intervention that can be considered in this type of situation is to work with a business to develop an orientation program for all new employees. If the orientation was a good idea, others will benefit from it as well.

Can't a substantial level of work competence compensate for cultural "deviance"? According to the "competence/deviance" hypothesis, initially developed by Marc Gold (1980), a certain amount of competence can counteract or neutralize an individual's deviance. One can improve in either area – either build competence or reduce deviance – and achieve a positive result. So, according to this hypothesis, an employee could concentrate solely on building excellent work skills, giving little thought to culturally normative behavior, and still be viewed as fitting in, in the sense of being regarded as non-deviant.

There is a great deal of merit in focusing on helping people gain competencies rather than on removing deviancies. And many aspects of cultural inclusion do involve building competencies. Learning to take one's turn asking co-workers if they want coffee, collecting money, and purchasing coffee at the cafeteria is an example of a breaktime custom (element #9) that involves significant competencies. But some elements of culture – for instance, whether one's work schedule is the same as one's co-workers' – do not require any specific competencies. It is unlikely that any amount of competency can neutralize or overcome the effects of poor inclusion into these elements of the culture.

The competence/deviance hypothesis has never been verified. It is not clear how it ever could be verified, because of the enormous difficulty that would be involved in measuring units of competence and units of deviance in a reliable way. And the hypothesis seems contraindicated by facts familiar to most people. Historically, people who found themselves discriminated against because something about them was viewed as deviant – African Americans in the days of racial segregation for example, or Jewish people in Nazi Germany – could not escape their deviant image by being especially competent. Great scientists, inventors, and philosophers were subjected to the same treatment as others.

A better way to look at it is to regard both "competence" and "deviance" as socially constructed realities. Unless one fits in with or becomes accepted by a social group to some degree, one can never begin to be seen as competent. There is no such thing as pure "competence," outside of a cultural context. Competence depends on inclusion, so there is no alternative to focusing seriously on cultural inclusion.

What about people who like being isolated or don't want to fit in? Is it possible for an employee to aim at a low inclusion score? Shouldn't a person have that choice? Not being social is different from not fitting in. We sometimes mix these two concepts together because so many cultural norms and customs relate to social interaction, for the simple reason that most people like being social. But not everyone. And workplace cultures can be found where people are customarily isolated much of the time. Someone who enjoys isolation would fit in well. And if the percentage of "yes" matches (rather than the absolute number) is used as a measure, the individual who enjoys having only occasional interactions would receive a high inclusion score.

There are individual exceptions to the general rule that cultural inclusion contributes significantly to job satisfaction. For instance, someone might enjoy a type of work so much that it matters very little to the individual whether co-workers are accepting or view the individual as fitting in. In this rare type of situation, a low level of inclusion does not automatically indicate a need to improve inclusion or terminate the job. But remember that inclusion in a workplace culture does contribute to job support, and job support is linked to job maintenance and success. So, with rare exceptions, workers will be more successful and have a higher quality of life the more we are able to understand and facilitate inclusion in workplace cultures.

References

Adkins, C. (1995). Previous work experience and organizational socialization: A longitudinal examination. *Academy of Management Journal*, 38, 839-862.

Akabas, S. (1994). Workplace responsiveness: Key employer characteristics in support of job maintenance for people with mental illness. *Psychosocial Rehabilitation Journal*, 17, (3), 91-101.

Balser, R., Harvey, B., and Hornby, H. (1998). Building employer support for hiring persons with psychiatric disabilities. *Mental Health*, 21(4), 2-4.

Barron, J., Berger, M., and Black, D. (1997). *On the Job Training*. Kalamazoo, MI: Upjohn Institute for Employment Research.

Butterworth, J., Hagner, D., Helm, D., and Whelley, T. (1999). The relationship between workplace culture characteristics and the social interactions, supports, and participation of transition-aged young adult (manuscript in review).

Campion, M., Charaskin, L., and Stevens, M. (1994). Career-related antecedents and outcomes of job rotation. *Academy of Management Journal*, 37, 1518-1542.

Darrah, C. (1994). Skill requirements at work: Rhetoric vs. reality. *Work and Occupations*, 21 (1), 64-84.

Darrah, C. (1995). Workplace training, workplace learning: A case study. *Human Organization*, 54, 31-41.

Dwyer, T. (1991). Humor, power, and change in organizations. *Human Relations*, 44 (1), 1-19.

Federico, P. (1995). Expert and novice recognition of similar situations. *Human Factors*, 37, 105-122.

Ferris, G. and King, T. (1993). Politics in human resources decisions: A walk on the dark side. *Organizational Dynamics*, 22, 59-70.

Galpin, T. (1995). Pruning the grapevine. *Training and Development Journal*, 49 (4), 28-33.

Garrick, J. (1998). Informal learning in corporate workplaces. *Journal of Human Resource Development*, 9, 129-144.

Gold, M. (1980). *Did I Say That?* Champaign, IL: Research Press.

Graham, L. (1993). Invisible man. In J. Epstein and R. Atwan (Eds.) *Best American Essays*. New York: Ticknor and Fields.

Hagner, D. (1989). *The Social Integration of Supported Employees: A Qualitative Study*. Syracuse, NY: Syracuse University Center on Human Policy.

Hagner, D. and DiLeo, D. (1993). *Working Together: Workplace Culture, Supported Employment, and Persons with Disabilities*. Cambridge, MA: Brookline.

Hagner, D. and Faris, C. (1994). *Inclusion and Support in the Workplace, Naturally*. Paper presented at the Annual Conference of the Association for Persons with Severe Handicaps, Atlanta, GA.

Hall, D. and Parker, V. (1993). The role of workplace flexibility in managing diversity. *Organizational Dynamics*, 22, 5-18.

Hanley-Maxwell, C., Bordieri, J., and Merz, M. (1996). Supporting placement. In E. Szymanski and R. Parker (Eds.) *Work and Disability: Issues and Strategies in Career Development and Job Placement*. Austin, TX: Pro-Ed.

Hansen, C. and Kahnweiler, W. (1993). Storytelling: An instrument for understanding the dynamics of corporate relationships. *Human Relations*, 46, 1391-1407.

Harrison, D., Price, K., and Bell, M. (1998). Beyond relational demography: Time and the effects of surface and deep level diversity on work group cohesion. *Academy of Management Journal*, 41, 96-107.

Hatch, M. (1993). The dynamics of organizational culture. *Academy of Management Review*, 18, 657-693.

Henning, P. (1998). Ways of learning: An ethnographic study of the work and situated learning of refrigerator service technicians. *Journal of Contemporary Ethnography*, 27, 85-136.

Hood, E., Test, D., Spooner, F., and Steele, R. (1996). Paid co-worker support for individuals with severe and multiple disabilities. *Education and Training in Mental Retardation and Developmental Disabilities*, 31, 251-265.

Kennedy, M. (1980). *Office Politics: Seizing power, Wielding Clout.* New York: Warner.

Johnson, J. (1995). *Improving On-the-Job Training.* New York: Amacom.

Koerner, B. (1998). Into the wild unknown of workplace culture: Anthropologists revitalize their discipline. *US News and World Report*, August 10, 1998, 56.

Lee, M., Storey, K., Anderson, J., Goetz, L., and Zivolich, S. (1997). The effect of mentoring versus job coach instruction on integration in supported employment settings. *Journal of the Association for Persons with Severe Handicaps*, 22, 151-158.

Lin, N. and Dumin, M. (1986). Access to occupations through social ties. *Social Networks*, 8, 365-385.

Locher, A. (1988). Appraisal trends. *Personnel Journal*, 67 (9), 139-143.

MacDonald, C. and Sirianni, C. (Eds.). *Working in the Service Society.* Philadelphia: Temple University Press.

Mank, D., Cioffi, A., and Yovanoff, P. (1997). Analysis of the typicalness of supported employment jobs, natural supports, and wage and integration outcomes. *Mental Retardation*, 35, 185-197.

McLaughlin, C., Garner, J., and Callahan, M. (1986). *Getting Employed, Staying Employed.* Baltimore: Brookes.

Moos, R. and Insel, P. (1974). *Work Environment Scale.* Palo Alto, CA: Consulting Psychologists Press.

Morey, N. and Luthans, F. (1991). The use of dyadic alliances in informal organization: An ethnographic study. *Human Relations*, 44, 597-613.

Morrison, E. (1993). Newcomer information seeking: Exploring types, modes, sources, and outcomes. *Academy of Management Journal*, 36, 557-589.

Nietupski, J., Murray, J., Chappelle, S., Strang, L., Steele, P., and Egli, J. (1993) *Dispersed Heterogeneous Placement: A Model for Transitioning Students with a Wide Range of Abilities to Supported Employment.* Iowa City, IA: Iowa University Affiliated Program.

Parent, W., Kregel, J., Wehman, P., and Metzler, H. (1991). Measuring the social integration of supported employment workers. *Journal of Vocational Rehabilitation*, 1, 35-49.

Pfeffer, J. (1998). *The Human Equation: Building Profits by Putting People First.* Cambridge, MA: Harvard Business School Press.

Pierce, J. (1996). Reproducing gender relations in large law firms: The role of emotional labor in paralegal work. In C. MacDonald and C. Sirianni (Eds.) *Working in the Service Society.* Philadelphia: Temple University Press.

Pitt-Catsouphes, M, and Mirvis, P. (1994). *The Work-Family Corporate Environment Scan.* Boston MA: Boston University Center on Work and Family.

Rafaeli, A., Dutton, J., Harquail, C., and Mackie-Lewis, S. (1997). Navigating by attire: The use of dress by female administrative employees. *Academy of Management Journal*, 40, 9-45.

Rafaeli, A. and Pratt, M. (1993). Tailored meanings: On the meaning and impact of organizational dress. *Academy of Management Review*, 18 (1), 32-55.

Reiter, E. (1996). *Making Fast Food: From the Frying Pan into the Fryer.* Montreal: McGill University Press.

Rothwell, W. and Kazanas, H. (1994). Improving On-the-Job Training: How to Establish and Operate a Comprehensive OJT Program. San Francisco: Jossey-Bass.

Sandelands, L., Glynn, M., and Larson, J. (1991). Control theory and social behavior in the workplace. *Human Relations*, 44, 1107-1130.

Sheldon, J. and Trach, J. (1998). Social Security Disability Insurance and Supplemental Security Income work incentives with recommendations for policy change. *Journal of Applied Rehabilitation Counseling*, 29 (4), 18-25.

Silliker, A. (1991). The role of social contacts in the successful job search. *Journal of Employment Counseling*, 30, 25-34.

Stern, P. and Kaloff, L (1996). *Evaluating Social Science Research*. New York: Oxford University Press.

Thomas, R. (1991). *Beyond Race and Gender: Unleashing the Power of Your Total Work-force by Managing Diversity*. New York: Amacom.

Trach, J., Beatty, S., and Shelden, D. (1998). Employers' and service providers' perspectives regarding natural supports in the work environment. *Rehabilitation Counseling Bulletin*, 41, 293-312.

Wanous, J. (1992). *Organizational Entry: Recruitment, Selection, Orientation, and Socialization of Newcomers*. Reading, MA: Addison Wessley.

Wayne, S. and Liden, R. (1995). Effects of impression management on performance ratings: A longitudinal study. *Academy of Management Journal*, 38, 232-260.

Wellins, R. and George, J. (1991). The key to self-directed work teams. *Training and Development Journal*, 21, 26-31.

Appendix

The Workplace Culture Survey

A. Strength of Workplace Culture

1. Have most of the workers been with the company for a year or more?

2. Are there some tasks that two or more workers perform together?

3. Are there certain tasks at work that almost everyone does?

4. Are co-workers generally available to give help or support if a worker has a problem?

5. Is there a set work schedule?

6. Is there a time during the work shift when it is easier or more likely for workers to talk socially?

7. Are there particular "gathering places" where workers are more likely to talk socially?

8. Do workers eat lunch (or other meal) at the same time?

9. Are there other breaktimes shared by co-workers?

10. Does the company provide a formal orientation for new workers?

11. Are specific arrangements made for employee training, such as pairing a new worker with a co-worker?

B. Level of Workplace Inclusion

1. Has the employee been with the company for a year or more?

2. Does the employee work on some tasks together with one or more co-workers?

3. Does the employee's job include those tasks at work that almost everyone does?

4. Are co-workers available or close by enough to give help or support if the employee has a problem?

5. Does the employee's work schedule match that of others in the work area or department?

6. Does the employee work during times when it is easier or more likely for workers to talk socially?

7. Does the employee have access to gathering places at appropriate times?

8. Does the employee eat lunch (or other meal) with co-workers?

9. Does the employee share breaktimes with co-workers?

10. Does or did the employee participate in formal orientation provided by the company for new workers?

11. Does or did the employee receive training by being paired with a co-worker, or other typical arrangement?

A. Strength of Workplace Culture

12. Do workers typically play some kind of prank on a new employee as a kind of initiation?

13. Are there special terms or language used by the workers?

14. Are any items issued to employees (e.g. locker, key, uniform, tools)?

15. Is there any equipment that workers share the use of?

16. Is there a particular code of dress or appearance for employees?

17. Are workers' names displayed, such as on mailboxes, doors, or a posted schedule?

18. Do workers personalize their work space with posters, coffee mugs, or other articles?

19. Do employees sometimes talk socially during work time?

20. Are there particular social customs workers follow, such as taking turns making coffee?

B. Level of Workplace Inclusion

12. Was an initiation prank played on the employee?

13. Does the employee know and use the special worksite terms or language?

14. Does the employee have items typically issued to employees (e.g. locker, key, uniform, tools)?

15. Does the employee's job include using the equipment that workers share?

16. Does the employee follow the same code of dress and appearance as others?

17. Is the employee's name included on mailboxes, doors, posted schedules, etc.?

18. Is the employee's work space personalized in some way?

19. Does the employee sometimes talk socially with one or more co-workers during work time?

20. Does the employee follow informal worksite social customs, (such as taking turns making coffee)?

A. Strength of Workplace Culture

21. Are there staff or employee meetings?

22. Is worker job performance formally reviewed by the supervisor?

23. Is there a typical routine for distributing pay within the work area or department?

24. Do workers celebrate any special occasions, such as birthdays?

25. Does the company sponsor any social activities, like an annual picnic, or any sports teams?

26. Do workers ever get together as a group before or after work or on their days off?

27. Does the company sponsor or assist with an Employee Assistance Program or wellness program?

28. Does the company assist employees with car pooling or provide public transit discounts or similar transportation assistance?

B. Level of Workplace Inclusion

21. Does the employee attend and/or participate in staff or employee meetings?

22. Is the employee's job performance formally reviewed by the supervisor in the same way as others'?

23. Does the employee receive pay in the same way as other workers?

24. Does the employee participate in workplace celebrations such as birthdays?

25. Does the employee participate in company-sponsored social activities such as an annual picnic or sports team?

26. Does the employee participate in get-togethers outside of work?

27. Does the employee use or have access to an Employee Assistance Program or wellness Program?

28. Does the employee use or have access to company-sponsored car pooling, public transit discounts or similar assistance?

A. Strength of Workplace Culture

29. Does the company utilize any employee incentives or awards programs?

30. Do company policies include any supportive work/family programs such as flextime or dependent care assistance?

31. Is there evidence of advancement or promotion of some workers from entry level to higher positions within the company

B. Level of Workplace Inclusion

29. Does the employee receive or have access to any employee incentives or awards?

30. Does the employee use or have access to company work/family programs?

31. Is the employee able to advance to higher positions within the company?

About the Author

David Hagner, Ph.D., serves as rehabilitation projects director with the University of New Hampshire Institute on Disability and co-director of the New England Regional Continuing Education Program for Community Rehabilitation Personnel. He has been involved in a number of supported employment research and demonstration projects and has written several publications related to employment and rehabilitation.